You're Fired

Now You Know What Whistleblowers Feel Like

Dedication

This book is dedicated to the thousands of whistleblowers, past and present. With courage, you disclosed fraud, waste, abuse and patient care issues. All of you have jeopardized your employment, many lost their jobs, and some had their careers destroyed. Because of your valor, each whistleblower can take satisfaction that you have made a positive influence.

Contents

Foreword

During the darkest hours of our country, in the harshest corners of the Earth, our Veterans served and sacrificed to provide us a blanket of freedom, safety, and well-being. Their sacrifices and the sacrifices of their families are unmeasurable and are debts that cannot be repaid.

Many Veterans are proud and selfless, and often do not complain of their physical or psychological pain. After their return from the battlefields of Afghanistan, Iraq, Vietnam, or from other unknown battlefields and duty stations, Veterans go through life with pain which is often ignored, and they are provided inadequate care while under the watch of our very own Veterans Administration.

The Senior Leadership at the VA often disregards reports and disclosures made by doctors, nurses, and other employees about the irrefutable, substandard care that our Veterans receive. Furthermore, the VA leadership continues to retaliate against whistleblowers who report these injustices. Dr. Klein and other honest VA employees are often terminated for reporting fraud, waste, and abuse - which is a direct violation of the law.

The VA management, at all levels, disrespects our Veterans to whom we owe so much. Unfortunately, they harass, blackball, terminate and retaliate against Whistleblowers, like Dr. Klein, who come to aid our Veterans.

These wrongdoers must be held accountable, and our great country must restore the honor we owe our Veterans.

Natalie Khawam, Esq., MBA, MS
Whistleblower Law Firm

Preface

"The message is clear that we will not tolerate whistleblower retaliation in the Department of Veterans Affairs."[1]

Department of Veterans Affairs Secretary Dr. David Shulkin

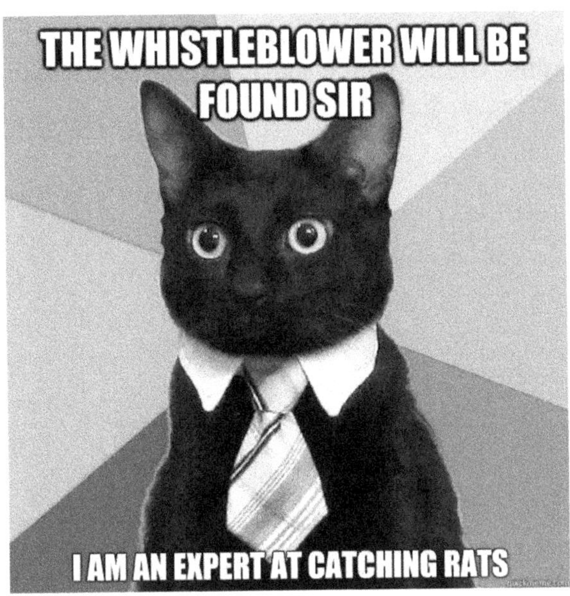

There are literally thousands of employees each year who blow the whistle on fraud, waste, abuse and substandard care within the federal government. On paper, there are many laws that should protect whistleblowers, most notable, the mythological avatar, "Whistleblower Protection Enhancement Act". Unfortunately, many whistleblowers face retaliation after making disclosures. Despite the risk of almost certain reprisal, fortunately for taxpayers, brave employees continue to step forward and report wrongdoing.

One such whistleblower case is reported in the pages that follow. The whistleblowers, made an anonymous disclosure to the Office of Inspector General, which ultimately led to the downfall of the Secretary of the VA, a cabinet level position, of the second largest department within the federal government.

It's ironic, that from the beginning of David Shulkin's tenure as VA Secretary, he made it clear, whistleblower retaliation would not be tolerated. Poetic justice prevails that whistleblowers, made incriminatory disclosures about Secretary Shulkin which led to his demise. The following pages describe Shulkin's retaliatory responses to the disparaging disclosures made by brave whistleblowers.

The whistleblowers' names remain anonymous. The names of others will be revealed within the narrative of this book which is based on true stories as reported in the news media.

While writing this manuscript, I purposely refrained from making political statements. Nor am I aligning myself with Democrats or Republicans. Veterans' affairs should be apolitical. After reading this paperback, you can make an informed decision about the topics which are discussed and dissected and the facts that are presented.

The last word of the last chapter in my book, *Scandals: Unmasking the Underbelly of the VA*, is "Hmmm". The first word in the first chapter of this book is "Hmmm". Reading *Scandals* is not a prerequisite for understanding this book. But the background presenting in *Scandals*, will provide insight of the shenanigans that occur in the federal government, especially the Department of Veterans Affairs, which sadly appear to be standard operating procedure.

---

[1] VA Secretary David Shulkin's quote at a White House briefing about President Trump's Executive Order; re: Whistleblower Protection Act. April 2017

Chapter One

Anonymous Whistleblowers' Letter

***"Getting these whistleblowers to understand that they're part of fixing the VA has been part of the progress that we're making."*[1]**

David Shulkin

David Shulkin
VA Secretary

Hmmm. Secretary David Shulkin's mantra from the first day on the job, was that he encouraged whistleblowers to come forward and he would protect them. And hold accountable VA employees who violated the rules, to include himself.[2]

On February 19, 2017, Secretary Shulkin did a wide-ranging on-camera interview with Pete Hegseth, FOX News Channel contributor. The interview appeared on *FOX and Friends* with the Secretary stating the following quote. *"Not only are we going to support those who tell us problems in the system, because that's how we get better, but we're going to address those problems."*

Countless whistleblowers took Shulkin's advice and did come forward by making disclosures about fraud, waste, abuse and substandard care. Unfortunately, those whistleblowers learned that they were not protected as promised.

I described extensively and in detail in my 2018 book release, *Scandals: Unmasking the Underbelly of the VA*, that despite multiple independent federal investigations ruling in my favor, Secretary Shulkin still allowed Dr. Klein to be terminated. For those readers who have not read my book, *Scandals*, the following is a brief synopsis.

The Poplar Bluff VA was built in the 1940's and had never had a pain management clinic. My first day on payroll with the VA was May 31, 2015. I was hired, to start from scratch, a pain management clinic. Shortly after I started work, it was obvious to me, administration was unsupportive of my goal to provide veterans standard of care in pain management. Hence, I made my first whistleblower disclosure in September 2015.

In March 2016, the VA abruptly closed the pain management clinic to silence me. The VA isolated me, and forced me to spend more than 16 continuous months sequestered in solitary confinement without assigned duties; as I stared at the walls in a small room. Despite the Office of Inspector General's investigation which substantiated every one of the many disclosures I made that they investigated. Despite the United States Office of Special Counsel's investigation that determined I'm a whistleblower and the VA retaliated against me. On August 22, 2017, the VA terminated my employment. To date, no definitive actions have been taken by the VA to correct the damages done to my career and reputation. Nor has the VA admitted to taking any punitive actions against administrators responsible for the retaliation. (Unless your definition of punitive includes one administrator re-assigned to another facility and another administrator retired a year earlier than he was planning to leave.)

The irony has not escaped me. Whistleblowers made allegations against David Shulkin regarding his European travel. Confirmation of those allegations, I believe will eventually lead to the Secretary's departure. Shulkin encouraged whistleblowers to disclose wrongdoing. And on television multiple times during his tenure, Shulkin expressed that he would hold accountable anyone who broke the rules. After reading this story, you can draw your personal conclusions if Dr. Shulkin got a taste of his own medicine.

On January 20, 2017, Donald J. Trump[3] was sworn into office as the 45th President of the United States. President Trump nominated David Shulkin as the Secretary of the VA. Mr. Shulkin was confirmed by the Senate on February 13, 2017.

A lot happened within the VA system after David Shulkin was confirmed by the United States Senate. Fast forward to November 2017, when a letter was sent by anonymous whistleblowers to Michael Missal, Director of the Office of Inspector General. That 10-page letter appears in its entirety below for you to read.

"November 12, 2017

The Honorable Michael J. Missal
Inspector General
Office of the Inspector General
Department of Veterans Affairs
810 Vermont Avenue, NW
Washington, DC, 20420

Dear Mr. Missal:

President Trump has indicated on numerous occasions that he will not tolerate the perception of wrongdoing by any of his immediate staff. We ask that someone please take a close look at the actions of his media savvy Secretary of Veterans Affairs David Shulkin. Since taking office, Secretary Shulkin has been quick to take the media stage and announce that he is firing someone based on VA 's New Accountability Law. However, to date he has not addressed his Chief of Staff [4] and previous Acting Under Secretary for Health Poonam Alaighn [5] M.D foreign travel trips and Prohibited Personnel actions, and illegal contracting for consulting services.

Here is some additional information that should be investigated:

Foreign Travel;

Secretary Shulkin has stated on several occasions that under his administration all employees will be held accountable for their actions. Therefore, he and his immediate staff should be held accountable for their expensive boondoggle foreign trip this past July. There was never a cancellation of scheduled meetings after the trip started. He and his staff planned to take at government expense, time to sight see while on this boondoggle. Do you really think that someone in the VA's Office of Ethics Counsel was going to disapprove his trip? There is no justification that can be made for this trip other than abuse of power and misuse of government funds. Also, Viveiva Simpson his Chief of Staff knew it was wrong because she stated that she did not want her husband James H. Simpson to go on the trip because of optics, that it was a boondoggle and would create a possible Office of Inspector General review.

This trip carries a stench of collusion to obtain under the table contracts with Danish, Swedish and British's official r s whom Shulkin, Vivieca Simpson and Poonam Alaighn met with behind closed doors at the Washington DC VA medical Center in September 2016.

1) Even though someone in the Secretary's Office lied and stated the Foreign Governments asked Shulkin to visit, this is the second meeting that Shulkin had with the Danish and Swedish business leaders. In fact, the same business leaders along with the Crowne Prince and Princess of Denmark visited the Washington, D.C. VA Medical Center in the fall of 2016.

2) The meeting had nothing to do with improving services to the Veterans it was all about how to develop strategies to sell Medical Devices and IT services to the VA Medical Centers nation-wide.

3) It was reported that the Crowne Prince and Princess stayed at the medical center less than 30 minutes and visited only two veterans. After which they quickly exited the facility while the business leaders had a private closed-door session with Shulkin the then Undersecretary for Health, his Chief of Staff, Vivieca Simpson and Special Assistant later Acting Under Secretary for Health, Dr. Poonam Alaigh. The business represented was medical records, supply chain management, IT, and medical supplies.

We refer to this meeting because it coincides with Shulkin's manufactured supply chain crisis at the Washington DC VA Medical Center in April 2017 when he fired the Director and got rid of anyone who had knowledge of this meeting. He then turns around and takes a trip to Denmark with his entourage, the same people that attended the September 2016 meeting with the foreign businessmen. This smells of impropriety and future kickbacks.

Please note none of the following former six living VA Secretaries ever took expensive foreign trips at VA expense or have been paid a salary higher than other Cabinet Members. David Shulkin continues to receive over per year the special salary approved by law under (38 U.S.C. 7306, 7404; section 30l(a) of Public Law 102?40) at Schedule 3 for the Under Secretary of Health for VA WM His Chief of Staff Vivieca Simpson coordinated within VA a sham that Shulkin would see patients via Tele-Medicine to maintain his Under Secretary of Health salary. This pay action was not approved by the White House or any Congressional Legislation. (There should be a hill of collection issued to Mr. Secretary)

Name	Term of office
Togo D. West, Jr.	1998-2000 **
Anthony Principi	2001-2005
Jim Nicholson	2005-2007
James Peake	2007-2009
Eric Shinseki	2009-2014
Robert A. McDonald	2014-2017

** Secretary West resigned due to an OIG investigation involving travel expenditures see VA OIG Report # 9AN-G83-I77, Dated 10-1-99

James Benjamin Peake MD was the sixth United States Secretary of Veterans Affairs, serving from 2007 to 2009. In 2004, he retired from a 38-year United States Army career. He also served as the 40th Surgeon General of the United States Army yet he did not receive a salary higher than other Cabinet Members Supreme Court Justices, Speaker of the House, Vice-President. Secretary Shulkin has continued to receive the same $367,500 salary that he received in FY 2017 by law as VA Under Secretary for Health which is approximately 165K over the level of current Cabinet Members, Congressmen, and Senator's and exceeds the Vice-President's and Supreme Court Justices salaries. There are other physicians in the President's Cabinet and the US House and Senate and they are not paid at the rate that Shulkin is paid. (Attachment 1 VA Contacts Document)

Prohibited Personnel Practices:

While Shulkin is boosting his own brand the Department is hurting specifically the Veterans Health Administration (VHA). VA continues to lose senior leaders due to retirement or fear of Shulkin retaliation and/or he and Vivieca Simpson's prohibited personnel practices in removing senior executives. (Attachment 2)

Simpson has also engaged in an illicit, immoral extra marital affair with another VA employee Marvin Cornish while in VA Headquarters'.

VHA has no permanent Under Secretary in fact the Acting Under Secretary for Health (same person who went on the trip with him) has resigned due to an OIG investigation.

Anyone who challenges Shulkin or Simpson on their illegal personnel practices is fired and trashed in the media just ask, Michael Culpepper, Scott Foster Bryan Matthews, Danielle Ocker, Brian Hawkins, James Schlosser, Diana Rubens, Leslie Wiggins, Dewayne Hamlin, Toby Matthews, Selma Vargas (OAR lead senior investigator) or any recently under investigation Senior Executive in the VA. (Attachment 3)

Secretary Shulkin's Chief of Staff Vivieca Simpson personally steered government consulting work to her friend/ previous supervisor who retired as a VA Healthcare Administrator.

In late 2016 Vivieca Simpson requested the services of William F. Feeley, a former Deputy Under Secretary of Health for Operations and Management for the Department of Veterans Affairs (VA) to mentor a 38 year career executive Steve Young (current Deputy Under Secretary of Health for Operations and Management for the Department of Veterans Affairs VA). Now Feelcy is currently mentoring the Acting Director at the Washington DC VA Medical Center at a rate exceeding $150.00 per hour since April 2017. There are no written progress reports from Feeley or the consulting firm for either project.

This is not the first contract that Vivieca Simpson has steered to retired VA Executives through Virginia-based Sinclair Advisory Group and Sigma Health Consulting LLC. At the top of the Sinclair Advisory Group is Stan Sinclair, former VA Deputy Under Secretary for Benefits VBA and Sigma Health Consulting LLC CEO, Frances Murphy who served as the Deputy Under Secretary for Health (DUSH) for Health Policy Coordination from 2002-2006 and as the Principle DUSH VHA from 1999-2002. These two firms are major recipients of VA consulting contracts many of them single-bid agreements that allowed for extensions sometimes worth more than the original contract.

Sinclair was the subject of a blistering Inspector General report in 2010 for receiving no-bid contracts from the VA, contrary to federal rules. "Sinclair and Sigma Health Consulting LLC Associates" who work through the companies to win government contracts are a Who's Who of former VA officials. Federal contracts generally must be competitively bid, except in certain special emergency situations. The head of an agency typically cannot pick an old friend to award a government contract. In this case, the situation is clouded.

We would like to pose this question to each of you; how can the Secretary of VA or his dogmatic Chief of staff pass moral judgement over other VA employees? They are currently under investigation by the 016 for committing erroneous travel practices which would be a terminal offense for any other employee especially Senior Executives. Their credibility is severely tarnished and yet they remain in positions of power to unjustly scrutinize dedicated career employees.

Employees in my office continue to have to defend this unethical, illegal and immoral behavior.

<u>Bewildered Veterans Affairs Employees</u>

cc:
Mr. Johnathan Alter
Ms. Danielle C. Belton
Mr. Nicholas Fandos
Senator Al Franken
Ms. Jacy Gomez
Congressman Trey Gowdy
Senator Lindsey Graham
Senator John McCain
Ms. Nicole
Senator Rand Paul
Senator Charles Schumer
Senator Elizabeth Warren
VA Executives - FYI

WASHINGTON DC VA CONTACTS
Gretchen Reinhardt

855-948-2311 White House VA Complaint Line. You will be asked for identifying information and then you can tell the person what your complaint is. You are supposed to receive a response with 14 days. Some vets do and some don't receive a reply. 8/2017

VA Secretary David Shulkin, David.Shulkin@va.gov 202-461-7000; US Dept of VA 810 Vermont Ave, Washington DC 20420 2016 $367,500 8/2017

Previous VA Secretary Bob McDonald, Robert.A.Mcdonald@va.gov Bob.Mcdonald@vs.gov cell# (513) 509-8454 SECVA Inquiry secvainquiry@va.gov

VA Deputy VA Secretary Scott R. Blackburn Scott.Blackburn@va.gov $168,700 8/2017

VA Deputy Secretary of Veterans Affairs - Thomas G. Bowman ThomasBowman@va.gov

VA Chief of Staff, Viveca Wright-Simpson Vivieca.Wright@va gov 8/2017

VA Executive in Charge, Veterans Health Administration Dr Carolyn M. Clancy Carolyn.Clancy@va.gov Phone: 202-461-0370 US Dept of VA 810 Vermont Ave, Washington DC 20420 FY 2016 $251,335 10/2017

VHA Client Services Response Team at VA Director of Client Relations, Debi Bevins Debi.Bevins@va.gov (202) 273-4816 Source: LinkedIn FY 2016 $153,702 8/2017

VA Inspector General Michael Joseph Missal michael.missal@va.gov $170,259 8/2017

VA Assistant Deputy Under Secretary for Health Clinical Operations, Dr. Thomas G. Lynch Tomas.Lynch@va.gov 202-461-7026 $302,918 8/2017

VHA Deputy Under Secretary for Health for Policy and Services (101?) Lucille Beck, Ph.D. Lucille. Beck@va.gov Phone: 202-461-7394 $177,966 8/2017

VHA Acting Assistant Deputy Under Secretary for Health for Patient Care Services (PCS) Harold Kudler, MD Harold.Kudler@va.gov $262,918 8/2017 Author of Sept article improving VA mental health care for Veterans starts with listening?

VBA, Director Office of Communications and Case Management (OCCM) David G. Spivey David.Spivey@va.gov not on FY 2016 federal salary file

VHA ADUSH for Access to Care Steven Lieberman, MD Phone: 202-461-7107 8/2017

VHA Chief Nursing Officer Linda McConnell MSN (lOAl) Phone: (202) 461-6700 8/2017 VHA Deputy Under Secretary for Health for Community Care Baligh R. Ychia, MD Phone: 202-461-4849 8/2017

VA Director, Office of Patient Centered Care online form email 8/2017

VHA Director, Office of Patient Centered Care irate} Cisudet, MD Phone: 202-266-4670 8/2017

VHA Acting Assistant Deputy Under Secretary for Health for Patient Care Svc. Harold Kudlen MD. Phone: (202) 461-7800 8/2017

VA Acting Secretary Veterans Benefits Administration, Dr. Tracy Gaudet; 202-266-4670; Tracy.Gaudet@va.gov

Principal Deputy Under Secretary Danny Pummiil, Danny.Pummill@va.gov 202-273-4816 VA Office of Accountability Review, not current

VA General Counsel Meghan Flanz, Meghan.Flanz@va.gov 202-461-7661 8/2017

VA Deputy Inspector General, Office of Inspector General, Linda Halliday; Linda.Halliday@va.gov (800) 488-8244 pay grade: ES - 00 8/2017

VA Public Affairs Officer Kristin Pressly, kristin.pressly@va.gov US Senator Ron Johnson (Wi) VA Whistleblower, Report Suspected Wrongdoing in VA Programs and Operations, vaoighotline@va.gov 800-488-8244

VA Special Security Officer, Pamela C. Prewitt, vanat@va.gov 202-461-5224 source: tine?. 8/2017

VHA Acting National Director for Pain Management, Dr Friedhelm Sandbrink, MD Friedhelm.Sandhrink@vagov source: https. Newsletter.samhsa.gov 2017 8/2017

Dr. Karen Drexler, M.D., the National Mental Health Program Director for Substance Use Disorders in the VA 8/2017

VHA Pain Management Program Coordinator, Pam Cremo; Pamela.Cremo@va.gov 203-937-3841 8/2017

VHA Clinical Pharmacy Specialist and Director, Jeffery.Fundin@va.gov

Program Director Principal Investigator Defense Veterans integrated Pain Management Dr Chester 'Trip' Buckenmaier

https://healthaffairs.org/blog/autho... 8/2017

Col US Army Ret cbuckenmsier@2 DVCIPM.org House Committee on Veterans AffairsWEBFORM:republican-veteransforms... house.gov/forms/writtencommittee/ VA Interim Assistant for Congressional and Legislative Affairs,

Chrisiopher.OConner@va.gov (202) 461-6490 Director of Congressional Legislative Affairs, VHA at Department of Veterans Affairs,

Crystal Ford; Crystal.Ford@va.gov House Office, Assistant Director, Congressional Liaison Service, Annmarie Amaral, B-328 Rayburn House Office Building US House of Representatives, Wash. 13.0, 20515; 202-225-2280; fax 202-453-5225

THE HONORABLE DAVID J. SHULKIN
U.S. SECRETARY OF VETERANS AFFAIRS
TRAVEL ITINERARY
COPENHAGEN, DENMARK LONDON, UK
JULY 11, 2017

<u>TRAVELING PARTY:</u>
Secretary Shulkin
Dr. Merle Bari, Spouse
Vivieca Wright Simpson, VA Chief of Staff
James 'Gabe' Cough, Director of Intergovernmental Affairs
Dr. Poonam Alaigh, Acting Undersecretary of Health (Will fly on separate flights)
Raman Alaigh, Spouse (GUEST) (Will fly on separate flights)
Assigned Security Detail

Tuesday, July 11, 2017

14:00-14:30   DEPART NEW YORK KENNEDY AIRPORT (JFK)

Wednesday, July 12, 2017

07:00 (CEST)   ARRIVE DENMARK

11:50-12:15   AMALIENBORG PALACE FOR CHANGING OF THE GUARD

13:30-14:30   CHRISTIANBORG PALACE SELF-GUIDED TOUR

16:00-17:00   COPENHAGEN CANAL TOUR FROM NYI-IAVN

17:00-17:40   WALK AROUND NYHAVN

18:00-19:30   VED STRANDER AND BAR

Thursday, July 13, 2017

09:00-09:05   MEETING & WELCOME W/DANISH MOD
                 By: Mr. Thomas Ahrenkiel, Permanent Secretary of State for Defense

09:05-09:25   BRIEFING 0N DANISH VETERANS POLICY HEALTH CARE
                 SYSTEM

09:25-09:45   BRIEFING ON THE ROLE OF THE DANISH VETERANS
                 CENTRE

10:45-11:15   VISIT THE VETERANS HOME

11:30-11:50   WREATI-I LAYING CEREMONY

12:30-14:15   LUNCH HOSTED BY DANISH MINISTER OF DEFENCE

14:30-15:30   GUIDED VISIT TO LOUISIANA MUSEUM OF MODERN ART,
                 HUMLEBKEK

16:00 - 17:15   FREDERIKSBORG CASTLE

19:00-20:30   DINNER AT NIMB BRASSERIE

20:30-21 :30   WALK TIVOLI AFTER DINNER

Friday, July 14, 2017

09:00-11:30   MEETING W/MINISTER OF HEALTH

11:45-13:30   ROUNDTABLE LUNCH W/CEO's 0F DANISH HEALTHCARE
                 COMPANIES

13:45-16:30   TOUR 0F RIGSHOSPITALET (Tour of research/teaching hospital)

16:45-18:00   STROGET

18:15-19:30   CAFE NORDEN

Saturday, July 15, 2017

08:30 (CEST)   ARRIVE LONDON/Heathrow, ENGLAND (LHR) AIRPORT

12:30-17:30   WIMBLEDON TENNIS TOURNAMENT

18:30-19:30   DINNER AT AL DUCA

Sunday, July 16, 2017

09:30-11:00   CHURCHILL WAR ROOM

11:20-11:35   BUCKINGHAM PALACE

13:15-14:45   KENSINGTON PALACE

11:45-12:25   WESTMINSTER ABBEY

16:00-17:00   THAMES RIVER CRUISE TO GREENWICH PIER

17:10-17:40   DINNER AT GREENWICHI FOLLOWED BYEVENING AT PICCADILLY CIRCUS

Monday, July 17, 2017

09:45-11:30   TOWER OF LONDON

11:40-12:40   TOWER BRIDGE

13:35-14:35   SHAKESOEARE'S GLOBE

14:55-17:40   EXECUTIVE WORK TIME

18:15-19:30   DINNER AT THE ARCHDUKE

19:45-20:15   LONDON EYE

21:15-22:15   CEREMONY OF THE KEYS

Tuesday, July 18, 2017

09:30-11:30   WINDSOR CASTLE

11:40-12:40   LUNCH AT COTE BRASSERIE

13:40-17:40   EXECUTIVE WORK TIME

17:45-18:00   WALK T0 10 DOWNING STREET

18:00-19:30   EVENING RECEPTION FOR SUMMIT DELEGATES GUEST

Wednesday, July 19, 2017

08:55-09:00	WELCOME OPENING ADDRESS By: Minister Ellwood (UK)
09:00-09:40	UK MENTAL HEALTH STRATEGY
09:40-10:40	VETERANS MENTAL HEALTH: FACTS, CHALLENGES
11:00-12:00	POST-TRAUMATIC STRESS DISORDER - SUICIDE - 20 min Presentation - 40 min Discussion David Shulkin, US Secretary of Veterans Affairs Dr. Poonam Alaigh, US Acting Undersecretary of Health
12:00-13:00	BARRIERS TO EFFECTIVE MENTAL HEALTH TREATMENT IN THE VETERAN POPULATION
14:00-1500	ALTERNATIVE THERAPIES (Cannabis, Service Dogs and Equine Therapy)
15:00-16:00	VETERAN CENTRIC REHABILITATION
16:00-17:30	MENTAL HEALTH CARE: THE UK APPROACH

Thursday, July 20, 2017

10:00-11:00	BRIEFING PRESENTATION
11:00-12:00	CONTINUUM 0F SUPPORT FOR TRANSITION FROM MILITARY SERVICE
13:00-14:00	TOUR OF ROYAL HOSPITAL CHELSEA BY THE GOVERNOR
14:00-15:00	REHABILITATION INITIATIVES 8c INTERVENIONS
15:00-16:00	ACCESS TO CARE FOR VETERANS
16:20-16:55	THE IMPORTANCE OF THE THIRD SECTOR
17:30-18:00	CONFERENCE CLOSING REMARKS NEXT STEPS

Friday, July 21, 2017

15:40 (BSN)	DEPART UK TO BALTIMORE WASHINGTON AIRPORT (BWI)
18:35 (EDT)	ARRIVE AT BWI AIRPORT"

Certainly, the above 10-page letter is a blistering description that does not make the upper echelon of VA leadership look good. Shortly after it became known the European excursion was going to be made public, the Undersecretary of Health, Poonam Alaigh, (who was on the trip accompanied by her husband) resigned.

Secretary Shulkin claims he did nothing wrong

Secretary Shulkin made the rounds with the news media. Shulkin reported that veterans should not worry that the trip complied with all ethics' rules and nothing inappropriate was done. Curt Cashour, VA press secretary, released on September 29, 2017, the following statement after the news broke about the Secretary's extensive entourage going on an extravagant 11-day multi-country vacation on the taxpayers' dime.

> **All of Shulkin's activities on the trip, including Wimbledon visit, "were reviewed and approved by ethics counsel," ***

*Curt Cashour, VA Press Secretary in a September 29, 2017 email explaining David Shulkin's European trek.

After the story broke in the news media, Secretary Shulkin did a video interview with a reporter from *The Washington Post* on November 9, 2017. During that interview, Shulkin fielded questions about the Wimbledon tennis event he and his family attended and gave specific answers that are archived in digital format for review. An excerpt of that transcript of *The Washington Post's* interview follows.

Secretary Shulkin: *"Well, this is your chance. Ask me any question you want."*

Reporter: *"Well, all right. The Wimbledon tickets."*

Secretary Shulkin: *"Yes?"*

Reporter: *"Did you buy those?"*

Secretary Shulkin: *"Yes"*

<u>Reporter</u>: *"Okay. So they weren't given to you as a gift by folks at the Invictus Games or anything like that?"*

<u>Secretary Shulkin</u>: *"No"*

Secretary Shulkin described himself during his tour of duty at the VA, as the person to fix the system by holding people accountable. Shulkin conveyed verbally and in writing that he would hold VA employees, <u>to include himself</u>, accountable for their actions. And he would not tolerate someone who does something to take the focus away from helping the veterans. In fact, during an on-camera interview on February 23, 2017 with Pete Hegseth, which was televised on *FOX & Friends*, Shulkin had the following quote. **Shulkin stated that Congress should, *"Hold the Secretary accountable. And that's what I really expect."***

After the European vacation in July 2017, Secretary Shulkin proceeded forward with scheduling/planning/preparing an official business trip with his wife to visit the Vatican.

---

[1] KTAR.com, January 5, 2018

[2] February 23, 2017 on-camera interview on *FOX & Friends* with FOX News Channel contributor, Pete Hegseth.

3

Donald J. Trump
President of the United States

4

Vivieca Wright Simpson
VA Chief of Staff, Washington DC

Poonam Alaigh
VA Undersecretary of Health

Chapter Two

Office of Inspector General Report

"We act with the highest ethical character,"[1]

David Shulkin

David Shulkin

The news of the European travel scandal by Secretary Shulkin and his large entourage quickly faded. However, just prior to Valentine's Day in February 2018, Donovan Slack, *USA Today* reporter, broke a story about an impending Office of Inspector General investigation that would be released later in the same week.[2] In Ms. Slack's article, she alerted the public that unfavorable information about Secretary Shulkin would be reported in the Office of Inspector General's report.

On February 14, 2018, the Office of Inspector General released to the public a 97-page report providing extensive and detailed accounting of Shulkin's European boondoggle. While preparing the report, the Office of Inspector General reviewed more than 12,000 documents and searched 493,000 emails. Additionally, the Office of Inspector General interviewed 28 individuals, to include the six-member security team assigned to protect Shulkin during his multi-country expedition.

Participants on this official U.S. government business trip were:
1) Dr. David Shulkin, VA Secretary
2) Dr. Bari (Shulkin's wife)
3) Poonam Alaigh, VA Undersecretary of Health
4) Poonam Alaigh's husband
5) Vivieca Wright Simpson, VA Chief of Staff
6) James Cough, VA Program Specialist
<u>Furthermore, there was a security detail of six (6) people</u>

For those of you who do not want to read the 97-page report in its entirety (which appears later in this same chapter), the follow section is the condensed Readers Digest version.

July 2017

SUNDAY	MONDAY	TUESDAY	WEDNESDAY	THURSDAY	FRIDAY	SATURDAY
9	10	11 Transit (after 2 p.m. EDT)	12 Arrive Copenhagen	13	14	15 Transit Arrive London (8.35 a.m. GMT)
16	17	18	19	20	21 Transit (1.15 p.m. GMT)	22

Figure 1. OIG analysis of trip calendar.

Scheduled official business[1]

Scheduled leisure

The table immediately above, depicts the scheduled official 11-day European business trip. During the 11 days in question, approximately 3.5 days were devoted to "*Scheduled official business*", which is signified by the darker blue color.

In the Office of Inspector General's official 97-page report, the following is a copy and paste:

> "*The OIG was able to determine that the trip cost VA at least $122,334. However, the OIG could not be more precise because VA's documentation was inadequate to assess the accuracy and appropriateness of the trip costs.*"

The following is another quote:

> "*To provide some relevant context, less than two weeks before the start of the trip, Secretary Shulkin issued a memorandum to all VA staff titled, **Essential Employee Travel**. The memorandum instructed staff that before approving any*

*employee travel, managers must determine whether the travel is "**essential**"
in order to decrease "employee travel and **generate savings**" within VA."*

Question: Was this 11-day luxury travel to multiple European vacation destinations "Essential"?

Question: Did 3.5 days of *"official business"* in Europe justify spending well north of $100,000 dollars?

Question: Was it necessary to pay for David Shulkin's wife's expenses on this trip?

Question: In this day and age of high-tech communications, was it necessary to travel to multiple European countries when communication technologies such as Skype, Facetime, video conferencing, etcetera exist?

The following are five eye-popping discoveries from the Office of Inspector General's report.

1. ***"VA's Chief of Staff* [Vivieca Wright Simpson]** *made false representations to a VA ethics official and altered an official record, resulting in VA improperly paying for Shulkin's wife's air travel"*

   "Since Mrs. Wright Simpson's false representations and alteration of an official record may have violated federal criminal statutes, the OIG referred this specific matter to the US Department of Justice (DOJ) to consider it for potential criminal prosecution;"

2. ***"Secretary Shulkin improperly accepted Wimbledon tickets"***

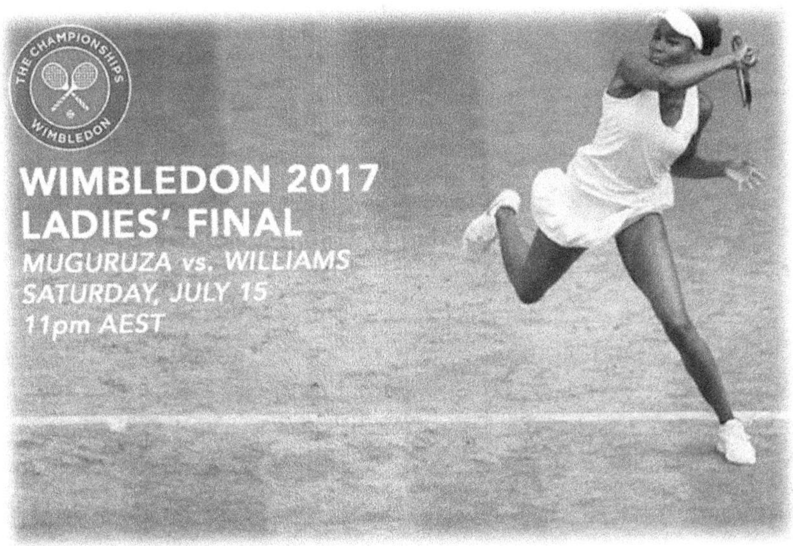

"Secretary Shulkin and Dr. Bari [Shulkin's wife] *attended the Ladies' Final tennis match at Wimbledon on July 15, 2017,"*

Secretary Shulkin accepted free tickets for the Wimbledon Ladies' Final tennis match from Victoria Gosling. Shulkin responded to an ethics official's question about the free tickets by stating the following.

> "Ms. Gosling was a friend of his wife and that "there is no business relationship, but purely a social friendship between the two of them."

> "The OIG separately analyzed the relationship between Shulkin's wife and Ms. Gosling and also determined that it would not meet the "personal friendship" exception because the gift was not given "under circumstances which make it clear that the gift [was] motivated by a family relationship or personal friendship rather than the position of the employee [emphasis added]." Accordingly, the Office of Inspector General found the acceptance of the Wimbledon tickets to be an improper gift."

3. **"Secretary Shulkin Directed the Misuse of a Subordinate's Official Time"**

> "The Office of Inspector General also determined that the Europe trip resulted in a misuse of VA resources."

The Office of Inspector General attained, reviewed and included in their meticulous report, communications/emails from Shulkin's wife, Dr. Bari, to a VA Program Specialist, James Cough. Information from one such email is shown below revealing Shulkin's wife requested a VA employee to schedule activities that she wanted to participate to include "*high tea*". And Shulkin's wife even sent the VA employee a PDF file of the restaurants that her husband, David Shulkin, likes to dine.

> "Dr. Bari's list of sites and activities to cover included Buckingham Palace, Westminster Abbey, the Churchill War Rooms, a Thames River cruise, London Eye, Tower Bridge, Tower of London (including the Ceremony of the Keys), Shakespeare's Globe, Trafalgar Square, Piccadilly Circus, St. Paul's Cathedral, Hyde Park, Kensington Palace, and Harrods. She also added events to consider, including Wimbledon, theatre tickets, day trips (to Stonehenge, Windsor, Bath), and high tea. She concluded her email with, "Thanks, I sent restaurants secretary liked under separate pdf.""

> "Prior to the trip, Secretary Shulkin directed VA Program Specialist Gough to work with Dr. Bari (Shulkin's wife) to plan personal activities for the Secretary and Dr. Bari during the trip. Emails support the conclusion that Mr. Gough made extensive use of official time for planning leisure activities. Mr. Gough effectively acted as a personal travel concierge to the Secretary and Dr. Bari.

> Personal activities planned for the Denmark trip included touring Amalienborg Palace for the Changing of the Guard; visiting Christiansborg

Palace, Rosenborg Castle, and Frederiksborg Castle; taking a boat tour of Copenhagen from Nyhavn Canal; and shopping in Copenhagen. There was also an unplanned excursion across the border to Malmo, Sweden, for dinner on their last day, July 14. For the London trip, planned tourist activities included excursions to the Churchill War Rooms, Buckingham Palace, Kensington Palace, and Westminster Abbey; a Thames River cruise; and visits to St. Paul's Cathedral, Tower of London (including the Ceremony of the Keys), Tower Bridge, Shakespeare's Globe, London Eye, and Windsor Castle."

In addition, Shulkin's wife was using the VA employee to try and get Wimbledon tickets for her and her husband. The Office of Inspector General included in their report the following communication.

"Although Secretary Shulkin ultimately obtained tickets to the July 15 Wimbledon Ladies' Final, Dr. Bari had also asked Mr. Gough about obtaining tickets to Wimbledon. Mr. Gough advised Dr. Bari on June 29 that he was attempting to use diplomatic connections to arrange Wimbledon tickets to the Gentlemen's Final for the Secretary and his wife: I'm asking ppl from the Embassy and the UK government about Wimbledon tickets and have not had much luck."

The Office of Inspector General concluded the Program Specialist, who Shulkin <u>ordered</u> to plan the <u>non</u>-business activities for him and his wife, spent an excessive amount of official VA time planning social events for the Secretary and his wife.

"This was time that should have been spent conducting official VA business and not for providing personal travel concierge services to Secretary Shulkin and his wife."

> **"Secretary Shulkin ignores his own stewardship obligations. "An employee shall not encourage, direct, coerce, or request a subordinate to use official time to perform activities other than those required in the performance of official duties or authorized in accordance with law or regulation." 5 C.F.R. § 2635.705."**

Rachel Maddow, MSNBC TV personality, provided an entertaining video to include pictures of the castles that Doctor Shulkin and his physician wife visited while on their European vacation funded by federal taxpayers.[3]

4. ***"Inadequate Documentation to Assess the Accuracy and Appropriateness of the Costs of the Trip"***

"The Office of Inspector General was able to determine that the trip cost VA at least $122,334. However, the OIG could not be more precise because VA's documentation was inadequate to assess the accuracy and appropriateness of the trip costs."

"There was also an inexplicable overpayment to one of the security personnel of $3,825 for parking."

5. **Misleading statements to the media**

*"On September 27, 2017, VA public affairs staff learned that The Washington Post was working on a story about the July 2017 Europe trip and that the reporters were seeking information from VA, including about Secretary Shulkin's attendance at Wimbledon. VA's Assistant Secretary for Public and Intergovernmental Affairs John Ullyot met with Secretary Shulkin about a response to the upcoming article. Mr. Ullyot told OIG investigators that Secretary Shulkin helped draft the response, including the sentence, "**All activities including Wimbledon were reviewed and approved by ethics counsel.**" **Secretary Shulkin denied having any involvement with the drafting of the response.**"*

*"Moreover, Secretary Shulkin was interviewed at a public forum by a Washington Post reporter on November 9, 2017. As part of that interview, Secretary Shulkin claimed that he paid for the Wimbledon tickets and that they were not a gift from "folks from the Invictus Games or anything like that." **That statement also is not accurate.**"*

According to the dictionary:
Lying (Adjective) *"Marked by or containing untrue statements."*[4]

Question: Did Secretary Shulkin lie to cover up his tracks about the 11-day luxury European travel escape for him and his wife which was paid for by federal taxpayers?

Question: Did VA leadership at the national level live up to Secretary Shulkin's quote, *"We act with the highest ethical character,"*?

Question: Do you think Secretary Shulkin should resign because of this scandal?

Question: Do you think President Trump should say, "You're Fired" to Shulkin because of this scandal?

Below is the 97-page Office of Inspector General's report in its entirety, which was released to the public on February 14, 2018.

Department of Veterans Affairs
Office of Inspector General

Administrative Investigation

VA Secretary and Delegation Travel to Europe

Report No. 17-05909-106
VA Office of Inspector General
Washington, DC 20420

February 14, 2018

EXECUTIVE SUMMARY

Administrative Investigation
VA Secretary and Delegation Travel to Europe

In April 2017, Secretary of Veterans Affairs David Shulkin accepted an invitation to attend the Ministerial Summit on Veterans' Affairs in London (London Summit). The purpose of the London Summit was to bring together senior officials from the United States, the United Kingdom, Canada, Australia, and New Zealand to discuss topical issues related to veterans. The London Summit began with a reception on the night of July 18, with meetings on July

19 and 20, 2017. After accepting the invitation, Secretary Shulkin asked his staff to arrange a visit to Copenhagen, Denmark. Working with US Embassy staff in Copenhagen and officials of the Danish government, meetings were scheduled for the morning of July 13 and on July 14. To conduct both visits, Secretary Shulkin led a VA delegation to the meetings in Copenhagen and London—leaving the United States on July 11 and returning on July 21, 2017.

After the trip concluded, the Office of Inspector General (OIG) received an anonymous complaint alleging that the trip was a misuse of VA funds because the trip included a significant amount of personal time, including Secretary Shulkin's attendance at the Wimbledon tennis tournament. The OIG conducted a thorough investigation that resulted in the findings and recommendations detailed in this report.

To provide some relevant context, less than two weeks before the start of the trip, Secretary Shulkin issued a memorandum to all VA staff titled, *Essential Employee Travel*. The memorandum instructed staff that before approving any employee travel, managers must determine whether the travel is "essential" in order to decrease "employee travel and generate savings" within VA. It was in this climate that the VA delegation for the Europe trip included Dr. Merle Bari, the Secretary's wife, who is a dermatologist in private practice; VA Chief of Staff Vivieca Wright Simpson; then Acting Under Secretary for Health Dr. Poonam Alaigh; and Program Specialist James (Gabe) Gough. Six members of the Secretary's security detail also went on the trip, with several additional days of advance travel. A VA Ethics Official approved Dr. Bari as an "invitational traveler," which authorized VA to pay her expenses. The trip cost VA at least $122,334.

The calendar below provides a summary of the planned official business and leisure time for the trip.

July 2017

SUNDAY	MONDAY	TUESDAY	WEDNESDAY	THURSDAY	FRIDAY	SATURDAY
9	10	11 Transit (after 2 p.m. EDT)	12 Arrive Copenhagen	13	14	15 Transit Arrive London (8:35 a.m. GMT)
16	17	18	19	20	21 Transit (1:15 p.m. GMT)	22

Figure 1. OIG analysis of trip calendar.

☐ Scheduled official business[1]

☐ Scheduled leisure

Secretary Shulkin told OIG investigators that he found the trip substantively valuable to VA's mission. While in Copenhagen, Secretary Shulkin and other members of the VA delegation had a number of meetings on issues related to Danish veterans' health issues and their healthcare system, participated in a roundtable lunch with CEOs of Danish healthcare companies, and visited a veterans' home and hospital. The joint communiqué of the London Summit noted that the delegates discussed a number of issues, including "post-traumatic disorder, rates of suicide and homelessness among veterans, barriers to mental health care, alternative therapies, veteran-centric approaches to the provision of services, and early intervention." Secretary Shulkin stated that he also worked on other VA matters during the trip when there were no official functions, which is corroborated by his handling of matters relating to a media crisis that developed relating to allegations of substandard care at the Manchester VA Medical Center. The group's schedule while in Europe, however, included significant personal time for sightseeing and other unofficial activities. While the OIG defers to Secretary Shulkin's determination as to the value to VA of the three-and-a-half days of meetings in Copenhagen and London, the OIG identified a number of serious derelictions concerning the trip, including the following:

1. VA's Chief of Staff Made False Representations to a VA Ethics Official and Altered an Official Record, Resulting in VA Improperly Paying for Dr. Bari's Air Travel

The OIG found that in April 2017 Chief of Staff Wright Simpson instructed staff to seek approval from VA ethics officials for Dr. Bari to be designated as an "invitational traveler." This would have authorized VA to pay her expenses on the trip. VA ethics officials initially declined to approve Dr. Bari as an invitational traveler on the grounds that the available information did not show that her presence would serve a "sufficient government interest." In response, Ms. Wright Simpson became personally involved and communicated directly with VA Designated Agency Ethics Official (DAEO) Tammy Kennedy. The OIG found that in order to obtain a favorable decision, Ms. Wright Simpson falsely represented to DAEO Kennedy that Secretary Shulkin would receive an award while in Denmark, which Ms. Wright Simpson understood to be the criterion that would justify Dr. Bari's travel at VA expense.[1] When Ms. Kennedy asked for additional information about the award that Ms. Wright Simpson told her would be presented to Secretary Shulkin, the following emails were exchanged:

- Ms. Wright Simpson to Program Specialist Gough: "Hey, when at the event in Denmark, will Dr. Shulkin be receiving an award or special recognition[?]"
- Mr. Gough immediately replied: "Not that I'm aware of. However, all of the planning is still in draft phase, and has not been finalized by Denmark."

---

[1] See *Travel Expenses to Attend Awards Ceremony—Spouse of Recipient*, 69 Comp. Gen. 38, 40 (Comp.Gen. October 26, 1989, interpreting 5 U.S.C. § 4503 to authorize payment of travel expenses for a federal employee's spouse to attend an award ceremony in which the employee is the recipient of an award presented by the agency. As detailed in the report, the OIG concluded that this guidance was inapplicable because there was no award being made by VA.

- Four minutes later, Mr. Gough sent another email to Ms. Wright Simpson: "We're working on having a dinner at the US Ambassador's Residence in honor of SECVA, but that has not been confirmed by US Embassy Copenhagen yet."

- Ms. Wright Simpson then altered this second email, making it appear that Mr. Gough wrote: "We're having a special recognition dinner at the US Ambassador's Residence in the honor of SECVA."

- Ms. Wright Simpson then forwarded the altered email to Ms. Kennedy with a note: "Let me know if you need more."

- Ms. Kennedy emailed in response: "Vivieca – This is exactly what I needed. Thanks. I am in the middle of drafting an e-mail which addresses the below and should serve as an approval to proceed."

The OIG found no evidence that Secretary Shulkin was aware of Ms. Wright Simpson's false representations or alteration of official records. Based on this email exchange and Ms. Wright Simpson's prior oral representation that Secretary Shulkin would be receiving an award, Ms. Kennedy approved Dr. Bari as an invitational traveler and VA paid more than $4,000 for her airline ticket. Ms. Kennedy told OIG investigators that she would not have approved the expense reimbursement for Dr. Bari if she had been informed that Secretary Shulkin was not getting an award. Secretary Shulkin did not receive an award or special recognition during this Europe trip. Dr. Bari also did not qualify for VA travel expense reimbursement under any other allowable criteria.

Since Ms. Wright Simpson's false representations and alteration of an official record may have violated federal criminal statutes, the OIG referred this specific matter to the US Department of Justice (DOJ) to consider it for potential criminal prosecution; DOJ decided not to prosecute at this time.

2. Secretary Shulkin Improperly Accepted Wimbledon Tickets

Secretary Shulkin and Dr. Bari attended the Ladies' Final tennis match at Wimbledon on July 15, 2017, which was the Saturday following the Copenhagen trip and four days before the London Summit meetings began. Secretary Shulkin told OIG investigators that he received tickets for the event from Ms. Victoria Gosling, whom he described as his wife's friend. According to publicly available information, Ms. Gosling is a UK resident and Head of Social Impact at Auden, a for-profit enterprise; a Military Director at Sage Foundation, the philanthropic affiliate of UK software company Sage Group plc; and a Military Councilor for the Lawn Tennis Association, which is the national governing body for tennis in Great Britain, including Wimbledon. Ms. Gosling also served as CEO of the 2016 Invictus Games held in Orlando, Florida.[2] Ms. Gosling not only provided the Wimbledon tickets, but she also hosted Secretary Shulkin, Dr. Bari, and their adult son for lunch before the match at the private

---

[2] The international Invictus games are "Prince Harry's sporting event for wounded, injured and sick Servicemen and women." (See https://invictusgamesfoundation.org.)

members' dining room at Wimbledon. OIG investigators made at least 19 attempts to contact Ms. Gosling between December 15, 2017, and January 24, 2018.

In a January 30, 2018 email response to the OIG's request for an interview, Ms. Gosling identified Secretary Shulkin and his wife as "friends of mine" and stated that she offered the tickets "to thank them for their personal support to me whilst I was CEO Invictus Games Orlando." In that email she agreed to talk with OIG investigators, but she did not thereafter respond to the OIG's efforts to schedule an interview. OIG investigators contacted her by telephone on February 6, 2018 and conducted an unscheduled interview. That interview confirmed Secretary Shulkin's account that prior to his acceptance of Wimbledon tickets, he and Dr. Bari only had contact with Ms. Gosling during three official events in the United States. During the course of the 26-minute interview, OIG investigators and Ms. Gosling referred to Dr. Bari only as Secretary Shulkin's "wife." Toward the end of the interview, OIG investigators asked whether Ms. Gosling could recall the first name of Secretary Shulkin's wife. After a long pause, Ms. Gosling was unable to recall Dr. Bari's name, stating, "You actually -- I think that kept throwing me. I'm actually having a genuine blank here." Ms. Gosling was unable to recall Dr. Bari's name before the interview concluded.

Federal ethics rules prohibit the solicitation or acceptance of any gift given because of the employee's official position or if the gift comes from a prohibited source, unless an exception applies.[3] Before accepting the Wimbledon tickets, Secretary Shulkin did not seek an opinion from VA ethics counsel as to whether it was appropriate to accept the tickets as a gift. On September 28, 2017, after being notified of a pending *Washington Post* story about the trip and the Wimbledon tickets, Secretary Shulkin asked VA General Counsel James Byrne to seek an expedited ethics review of his acceptance of the tickets. To conduct the analysis, DAEO Kennedy sent Secretary Shulkin a series of written questions. In response, Secretary Shulkin wrote that Ms. Gosling was a friend of his wife and that "there is no business relationship, but purely a social friendship between the two of them." Based on the responses to the questions, Ms. Kennedy opined that Secretary Shulkin could accept the tickets based on the "personal friendship" exception to the rule prohibiting the acceptance of gifts.[4]

The OIG determined that the information DAEO Kennedy obtained from Secretary Shulkin was insufficient to accurately describe his or his wife's relationship with Ms. Gosling. Dr. Bari first met Ms. Gosling in 2015 at a reception at the British Ambassador's residence and the two had met at two other official events, including the Invictus Games in Orlando. The OIG did not identify, nor did Secretary Shulkin provide, evidence of a relationship between Dr. Bari and Ms. Gosling sufficient to meet the "personal friendship" exception. The OIG presented the information developed during the investigation about the relationship between

---

[3] 5 CFR 2635.202.

[4] See 5 C.F.R. § 2635.204(b) ("An employee may accept a gift given by an individual under circumstances which make it clear that the gift is motivated by a family relationship or personal friendship rather than the position of the employee. Relevant factors in making such a determination include the history and nature of the relationship and whether the family member or friend personally pays for the gift.")

Dr. Bari and Ms. Gosling to DAEO Kennedy.[5] After reviewing this additional information from the OIG, DAEO Kennedy concluded, the "totality of the documents totally indicate that they're not friends, as represented in [Secretary Shulkin's] response to me." Ms. Kennedy told OIG investigators that, had she known this information at the time, she would not have given a favorable ethics opinion concerning the acceptance of the Wimbledon tickets. The OIG separately analyzed the relationship between Dr. Bari and Ms. Gosling and also determined that it would not meet the "personal friendship" exception because the gift was not given "under circumstances which *make it clear* that the gift [was] motivated by a family relationship or personal friendship rather than the position of the employee [emphasis added]."[6] Accordingly, the OIG found the acceptance of the Wimbledon tickets to be an improper gift.

Secretary Shulkin Directed the Misuse of a Subordinate's Official Time

The OIG also determined that the Europe trip resulted in a misuse of VA resources. While the delegation spent nine full days in Europe, there were only three-and-a-half days of meetings in addition to a reception the evening before the start of the London Summit. Prior to the trip, Secretary Shulkin directed VA Program Specialist Gough to work with Dr. Bari to plan personal activities for the Secretary and Dr. Bari during the trip. Emails support the conclusion that Mr. Gough made extensive use of official time for planning leisure activities. Mr. Gough effectively acted as a personal travel concierge to the Secretary and Dr. Bari.

Personal activities planned for the Denmark trip included touring Amalienborg Palace for the Changing of the Guard; visiting Christiansborg Palace, Rosenborg Castle, and Frederiksborg Castle; taking a boat tour of Copenhagen from Nyhavn Canal; and shopping in Copenhagen. There was also an unplanned excursion across the border to Malmo, Sweden, for dinner on their last day, July 14. For the London trip, planned tourist activities included excursions to the Churchill War Rooms, Buckingham Palace, Kensington Palace, and Westminster Abbey; a Thames River cruise; and visits to St. Paul's Cathedral, Tower of London (including the Ceremony of the Keys), Tower Bridge, Shakespeare's Globe, London Eye, and Windsor Castle.

The OIG was unable to determine the total amount of official time Mr. Gough spent planning these personal activities at the direction of Secretary Shulkin and Dr. Bari. However, it was clear from the extensive communications between Mr. Gough and Dr. Bari that he spent many hours attending to the personal aspects of the trip on their behalf that exceeded what was required to notify the security detail of their proposed movements. This was time that should have been spent conducting official VA business and not for providing personal travel concierge services to Secretary Shulkin and his wife.

---

[5] The OIG presented the information to Ms. Kennedy prior to the OIG's unscheduled interview with Ms. Gosling on February 6, 2018. At the time of the OIG's discussion with Ms. Kennedy, Ms. Kennedy knew that the tickets were provided to Secretary Shulkin and his wife by Ms. Gosling, but she did not have confirmation that Ms. Gosling had paid for the tickets herself. This additional information, learned from OIG's discussion with Ms. Gosling, does not change OIG's conclusion that the friendship exception is inapplicable.
[6] 5 CFR 2653.204.

Inadequate Documentation to Assess the Accuracy and Appropriateness of the Costs of the Trip

The OIG was able to determine that the trip cost VA at least $122,334. However, the OIG could not be more precise because VA's documentation was inadequate to assess the accuracy and appropriateness of the trip costs. The OIG did identify discrepancies and potential errors that warrant a closer examination by VA auditors. For example, VA requires travelers to provide a Travel Cost Comparison Worksheet, which compares the actual cost of the trip with the cost of the trip excluding personal travel expenses. No such worksheet was completed for this trip. The OIG found that personal conveniences did impact the cost of the trip. The travel itineraries of Secretary Shulkin, Dr. Bari, and five other members of the delegation departed earlier than previously scheduled from Copenhagen to London in order for the Secretary and Dr. Bari to attend Wimbledon. In addition to the $372 in travel agency transaction fees, this change also added $1,733 to lodging costs because VA paid for an early hotel check-in for six rooms, including for Secretary Shulkin and Dr. Bari. In another example of insufficient documentation, Ms. Wright Simpson's original roundtrip economy class airfare cost $1,101. However, her ticket was modified so that there was a different connecting city. This change increased the ticket price to $4,041. Travel records are insufficient to determine what justification, if any, was provided for this increased ticket price. There was also an inexplicable overpayment to one of the security personnel of $3,825 for parking and $2,718 for lodging.

3. Misleading Statements to the Media

The OIG further determined that VA issued a misleading statement to *The Washington Post* about the trip and did not correct the statement despite knowing that it was not entirely accurate. On September 27, 2017, VA public affairs staff learned that *The Washington Post* was working on a story about the July 2017 Europe trip and that the reporters were seeking information from VA, including about Secretary Shulkin's attendance at Wimbledon. VA's Assistant Secretary for Public and Intergovernmental Affairs John Ullyot met with Secretary Shulkin about a response to the upcoming article. Mr. Ullyot told OIG investigators that Secretary Shulkin helped draft the response, including the sentence, "All activities including Wimbledon were reviewed and approved by ethics counsel." Secretary Shulkin denied having any involvement with the drafting of the response. On the same day that Mr. Ullyot met with Secretary Shulkin, two ethics officials (one of whom was Ms. Kennedy) met with General Counsel Byrne to discuss, among other things, what ethics reviews pertaining to the Europe trip had been conducted. The ethics officials informed Mr. Byrne that the only activity reviewed by them prior to the trip was whether Dr. Bari could be included as an invitational traveler. Mr. Byrne told OIG investigators that the sentence included in *The Washington Post* story on September 28, 2017, was "generally true" and that he approved it to be released. However, he took no subsequent actions to correct it, even after VA ethics officials informed him that they did not believe it was an accurate statement because ethics officials had not reviewed "all" activities.

Moreover, Secretary Shulkin was interviewed at a public forum by a *Washington Post* reporter on November 9, 2017. As part of that interview, Secretary Shulkin claimed that he paid for the Wimbledon tickets and that they were not a gift from "folks from the Invictus Games or anything like that." That statement also is not accurate.

The OIG is recommending that (1) Secretary Shulkin reimburse VA for Dr. Bari's airfare; (2) Secretary Shulkin reimburse Ms. Gosling for the cost of the Wimbledon tickets and any other tangible benefits, and if she does not accept reimbursement, that he pay the same amount into the US Treasury; (3) VA take any appropriate administrative action against Ms. Wright Simpson and other individuals concerning the Europe trip; (4) VA audit the expense vouchers, travel authorizations, and the time and attendance records for all travelers and take any appropriate action to correct any errors; and (5) VA assess and enhance its training relating to the topics of travel planning, approvals, and the solicitation or acceptance of gifts.

MICHAEL J. MISSAL
Inspector General

Contents

Introduction

The VA Office of Inspector General (OIG) received an allegation from an anonymous source that Secretary of Veterans Affairs David J. Shulkin, VA Chief of Staff (COS) Vivieca Wright Simpson, and then Acting Under Secretary for Health Dr. Poonam Alaigh misused VA funds for travel to Europe and that the trip was more for personal than business reasons. Secretary Shulkin led a VA delegation to Copenhagen and London, leaving the United States on July 11 and returning on July 21, 2017 (Europe trip). The itinerary included a mix of business and tourist activities. The total cost paid by VA for the trip was at least $122,334.[7]

To assess this allegation, OIG investigators interviewed 29 individuals with knowledge of this matter, some on more than one occasion. Interviewees included Secretary Shulkin; Chief of Staff Vivieca Wright Simpson; then Acting Under Secretary for Health Dr. Poonam Alaigh; General Counsel James Byrne; Assistant Secretary for Office of Public and Intergovernmental Affairs John Ullyot; Assistant Secretary for Operations, Security, and Preparedness Donald Loren; Program Specialist James (Gabe) Gough; VA ethics officials; other VA staff involved in planning the trip; and Secretary Shulkin's six-member security detail who accompanied him on the trip. The OIG conducted searches of more than 493,000 emails and reviewed in excess of 12,000 documents. The OIG also reviewed various federal laws, regulations, and VA policy.

The Europe Trip

Secretary Shulkin told OIG investigators that he found the trip substantively valuable to VA's mission. While in Copenhagen, Secretary Shulkin and other members of the VA delegation had a number of meetings on issues related to Danish veterans' health issues and their healthcare system, participated in a roundtable lunch with CEOs of Danish healthcare companies, and visited a veterans' home and hospital. In London, Secretary Shulkin and other VA staff attended an international meeting of government ministers from four allied nations to discuss health issues facing veteran communities.

The OIG cannot determine the trip's value to VA, which is a decision that fits squarely within Secretary Shulkin's discretion. Excluding two travel days, the trip included three and-a-half days of meetings, an official evening reception, and five-and-a-half days of personal time. Secretary Shulkin told OIG investigators that he attended to his duties as Secretary even during the portions of the trip where the schedule reflected planned tourist activities. The

---

[7] The OIG identified at least $122,334 in direct travel costs related to the Europe trip. There are other direct and/or indirect costs as well, such as employee overtime for members of the security detail, and potentially others.

following is a summary of the trip and a description of the serious derelictions by VA personnel that occurred in connection with the trip.

Secretary Shulkin Accepted an Invitation to the Ministerial Summit on Veterans' Affairs in London, UK

In April 2017, the UK Parliamentary Under Secretary of State and Minister for Defense Personnel and Veterans invited Secretary Shulkin to attend the Ministerial Summit on Veterans' Affairs (London Summit) to be held July 18–20, 2017. The summit is held every 18–24 months to address challenges facing the veteran communities of Australia, Canada, New Zealand, the United Kingdom, and the United States.[8] Secretary Shulkin accepted the invitation.

The agenda for the London Summit began with a reception the evening of July 18 and was followed by two full days of meetings. The theme was "Future Support to Veterans and Mental Health." The joint communiqué issued after the summit stated that the delegates discussed a number of issues, including "post-traumatic disorder, rates of suicide and homelessness among veterans, barriers to mental health care, alternative therapies, veteran-centric approaches to the provision of services, and early intervention."

Secretary Shulkin Added Denmark to the London Summit Itinerary and Selected a Delegation to Accompany Him

After Secretary Shulkin accepted the invitation to attend the London Summit, he asked his staff in April to add Denmark to his July 2017 travel plan because he wanted to visit with Danish officials and learn more about their healthcare system. Secretary Shulkin told OIG investigators that he had at least three prior interactions with Danish government officials, and each time, they invited the Secretary to visit Denmark. Secretary Shulkin detailed that he first met with the Danish Ambassador and Crown Prince in 2016 when they visited the Washington DC VA Medical Center. Secretary Shulkin stated that he would not have made a special trip to Denmark, but the opportunity arose to have such a trip coincide with his travel to the London Summit.

Secretary Shulkin told OIG investigators that he felt Denmark offered important lessons to VA because of the similarities of the injuries suffered by Danish and US veterans, their technology, and the way they recently organized their healthcare system. He explained that Denmark had consolidated its government hospitals into centers of excellence. Secretary Shulkin said that a comparable reorganization of the VA healthcare system was on his agenda, due in part to the number of underutilized VA facilities.

---

[8] In 2014, the United States hosted the summit in West Point, New York. (See VA Press Release, "VA Hosts Senior International Forum and Ministerial Summit on Veterans Affairs" (April 8, 2014), https://www.va.gov/opa/pressrel/pressrelease.cfm?id=2535).

Mr. Gough was asked to assist with the planning and he worked with Danish and US Embassy officials in Denmark to determine a schedule for Secretary Shulkin's visit. In an email to a contact at the Royal Danish Embassy on April 18, 2017, Mr. Gough asked if

Secretary Shulkin could visit Denmark on July 12 and 13 to "say hello to the Crown Prince, and get a better understanding of the Danish health care system." In an email to members of Secretary Shulkin's staff on April 24, 2017, Mr. Gough wrote,

They are enthusiastic about hosting Secretary Shulkin in Denmark. They'd like to get a little better idea of his interests in the Danish Health Care System and if there is any location in particular he would like to visit? Anyone in particular he would like to meet? Topics he's most interested in? etc.

In an email to Mr. Gough on April 30, 2017, Secretary Shulkin asked whether the Denmark trip was confirmed for July 13 and 14 so that he could begin to make plans. He said, "Once you know please send me a note." Mr. Gough replied that he should have solid details by mid-week. The next day, a staff member wrote to Mr. Gough that Secretary Shulkin wanted confirmation of the Denmark trip by "tomorrow." Mr. Gough replied,

I can only work as fast as their embassy works. They have indicated they are excited for the [S]ecretary to go to Denmark, so I'm confident the trip over there is a go. They're still working on the details of the meetings / visits we would like. Those are what haven't been confirmed. I'm also working with them on a spousal itinerary.

Secretary Shulkin selected Ms. Wright Simpson, Dr. Alaigh, and Mr. Gough to accompany him on this trip, and subsequently, Secretary Shulkin's and Dr. Alaigh's spouses were added to the list of travelers (VA delegation).[9] Secretary Shulkin told OIG investigators that as then Acting Under Secretary for Health, Dr. Alaigh's attendance was necessary because the London Summit was focused on veteran healthcare issues, particularly mental health issues, and Dr. Alaigh was responsible for implementing related changes for VA and could speak to these issues. He said he selected Mr. Gough, as he was the person organizing and planning the intergovernmental aspects of the agenda. Secretary Shulkin further stated that he selected Ms. Wright Simpson because she would be able to understand and implement any administrative follow-up measures.

VA Approved the Request to Pay Travel Expenses for Secretary Shulkin's Wife

On June 1, 2017, Ms. Wright Simpson issued a memorandum estimating costs for the trip to be between $5,000 and $8,000 per traveler, inclusive of transportation, lodging, meals, and incidental expenses. She identified Secretary Shulkin, Dr. Bari, Ms. Wright Simpson, Dr. Alaigh, Mr. Gough, and seven security detail as approved to travel. (Only six of the security detail made the trip.) The air transportation cost was $25,478 when the tickets were initially purchased, but changes made to the airline reservations resulted in final air transportation costs of $42,230, which included $3,492 in travel agency change processing fees. VA paid $4,312

---

[9] VA paid the air transportation costs associated with Secretary Shulkin's wife, Dr. Bari. Dr. Alaigh did not seek reimbursement for any expenses associated with her husband's travel.

for Dr. Bari's air transportation and $10,498 for Secretary Shulkin's air transportation.[10] Dr. Bari did not seek reimbursement for meals and incidental expenses, although she had been authorized to do so. The trip ultimately cost VA at least $122,334.

Secretary Shulkin told OIG investigators that his wife had planned to pay for her own airfare and expenses, but that several days after advising his staff that Dr. Bari would accompany him, his staff told him that "VA was going to pay for her trip." It was Secretary Shulkin's recollection that his staff first suggested this possibility to him. He stated that it was preferable for VA to pay for her airfare "…so that we could travel together. Because what happens when she books her own airfare, and I do switch my tickets, she is stuck with an unusable ticket." Secretary Shulkin continued, "…staff told me about this. They told me that they had cleared it through ethics. I don't deal with those issues. So, I didn't question that." Mr. Gough told OIG investigators that while at a reception at the Colombian Embassy on April 27, 2017, Secretary Shulkin asked him if VA would be able to pay Dr. Bari's expenses for the Europe trip.[11] Mr. Gough said he advised Secretary Shulkin that the decision would need to be made by VA ethics officials, but that Mr. Gough would perform "due diligence to see if [the trip] met the requirements."

On or about May 2, 2017, the Office of General Counsel Ethics Specialty Team (Ethics Team) began its analysis of whether VA could pay for Secretary Shulkin's wife's travel expenses. The Ethics Team requested information from Secretary Shulkin's staff, which was not provided until June 2, 2017, when the VA Executive Travel Coordinator contacted the Ethics Team requesting a same-day determination as to the approval of the travel authorization request for the Secretary's wife.[12]

An Ethics Team attorney responded,

> I've reviewed this [request for invitational travel order concurrence for Dr. Bari] along with Tammy Kennedy (VA's designated agency ethics official), and we have not seen sufficient facts to determine that invitational travel orders

---

[10] Secretary Shulkin flew economy class to Copenhagen. However, he and a member of his security detail flew business class on the return trip from London to Washington due to a documented medical necessity by Secretary Shulkin. Federal travel regulations authorize an agent assigned to the Secretary's security detail to accompany him in business class. 41 C.F.R. § 301-10.123.

[11] The recollections of Secretary Shulkin and Mr. Gough appear to differ as to who first asked whether VA could pay Dr. Bari's travel expenses. May 1, 2017 planning emails between Mr. Gough and a colleague confirm that Mr. Gough had a conversation with Secretary Shulkin at the Embassy of Colombia relating to the trip and that up until that point the trip planners were operating under the assumption that Dr. Bari would pay for her own travel expenses. The OIG does not need to resolve this potential conflict because this fact is not material to the analysis.

[12] On May 25, 2017, a travel authorization was created for Dr. Bari by a Special Assistant involved in the trip planning. The Director of Administrative Operations approved it the same day. This approval was improper because the Office of General Counsel had not yet approved Dr. Bari's invitational travel, nor had she been officially invited. The error was detected in connection with arrangements being made to issue an Official Passport to Dr. Bari (US citizens traveling on official federal government business may not use their personal passports).

are permissible in this situation. Tammy has left messages with [a staff member] and the Chief of Staff seeking more details. As [Senior Ethics Attorney, Jonathan Gurland's] guidance indicates, VA may pay for a spouse's travel if the spouse's presence serves a "sufficient government interest." For example, if the employee is receiving an award or honor, or the travel results in a direct service to the Government…It's not clear, from the facts presented, that Dr. Bari's participation serves a "sufficient Government interest." From the facts we've received she will attend the events, which include health-care topics, but it does not appear that she is formally speaking or otherwise providing a direct service to the Government.

The VA Executive Travel Coordinator forwarded the Ethics Team attorney's email to Ms. Wright Simpson, adding, "per the message below from [the Office of General Counsel], it doesn't appear that VA can approve invitational travel orders for Dr. Bari's trip to Denmark/London. Standing by for further guidance." Ms. Wright Simpson responded that she would contact Ms. Kennedy.

The Chief of Staff Made False Representations to a VA Ethics Official and Altered an Official Record

Designated Agency Ethics Official (DAEO) Tammy Kennedy confirmed that on June 2, 2017, she had multiple telephone conversations with an Ethics Team attorney and they agreed that additional information was needed if VA were to approve the request for Dr. Bari's invitational travel. Based upon the information available, their analysis could identify no direct benefit to VA, and therefore approval could not be granted.

Ms. Kennedy told OIG investigators that when she spoke with Ms. Wright Simpson, she described permissible bases upon which the request must be founded. She stated that one such basis included spousal attendance at an event where the Secretary would be receiving an award or honor.[13] Ms. Kennedy stated that during the call-in response to this information, Ms. Wright Simpson said that Secretary Shulkin was in fact receiving an award from the US Ambassador to Denmark. Ms. Kennedy told OIG investigators that Ms. Wright Simpson sounded "confident" in her statement that Secretary Shulkin was receiving an award from the US Ambassador in Denmark. Ms. Kennedy stated that Ms. Wright Simpson also represented to her that Secretary Shulkin's travel to Europe, including Dr. Bari's travel, was "approved by the White

---

[13] The OIG does not adopt Ms. Kennedy's legal conclusion that VA may pay for an employee's spouse to accompany him or her to accept an award from an organization other than VA.

House," but Ms. Wright Simpson could not recall the name of the individual at the White House who approved the trip.[14]

On that same day, shortly after making the oral representation to Ms. Kennedy that Secretary Shulkin was expected to receive an award, the following emails were exchanged:

- Ms. Wright Simpson to Program Specialist Gough: "Hey, when at the event in Denmark, will Dr. Shulkin be receiving an award or special recognition[?]"
- Mr. Gough immediately replied: "Not that I'm aware of. However, all of the planning is still in draft phase, and has not been finalized by Denmark."

- Four minutes later, Mr. Gough sent another email to Ms. Wright Simpson: "We're working on having a dinner at the US Ambassador's Residence in honor of SECVA, but that has not been confirmed by US Embassy Copenhagen yet."[15]

- Ms. Wright Simpson then altered this second email, making it appear that
Mr. Gough wrote: "We're having a special recognition dinner at the US
Ambassador's Residence in the honor of SECVA."

- Ms. Wright Simpson then forwarded the altered email to Ms. Kennedy with a note: "Let me know if you need more."

- Ms. Kennedy emailed in response: "Vivieca – This is exactly what I needed. Thanks. I am in the middle of drafting an e-mail which addresses the below and should serve as an approval to proceed."

The original email Mr. Gough sent to Ms. Wright Simpson and the altered email are depicted here.

---

[14] Ms. Wright Simpson denied that she told Ms. Kennedy that the White House approved Dr. Shulkin's travel. Ms. Kennedy's contemporaneous notes of her conversation with Ms. Wright Simpson make reference to a representation by Ms. Wright Simpson that the White House approved the travel.

[15] Mr. Gough stated that these two emails were the only communications he had with Ms. Wright Simpson about a reception in Denmark.

Original Email sent from Mr. Gough to Ms. Wright Simpson   Altered Email sent from Ms. Wright Simpson to Ms. Kennedy[16]

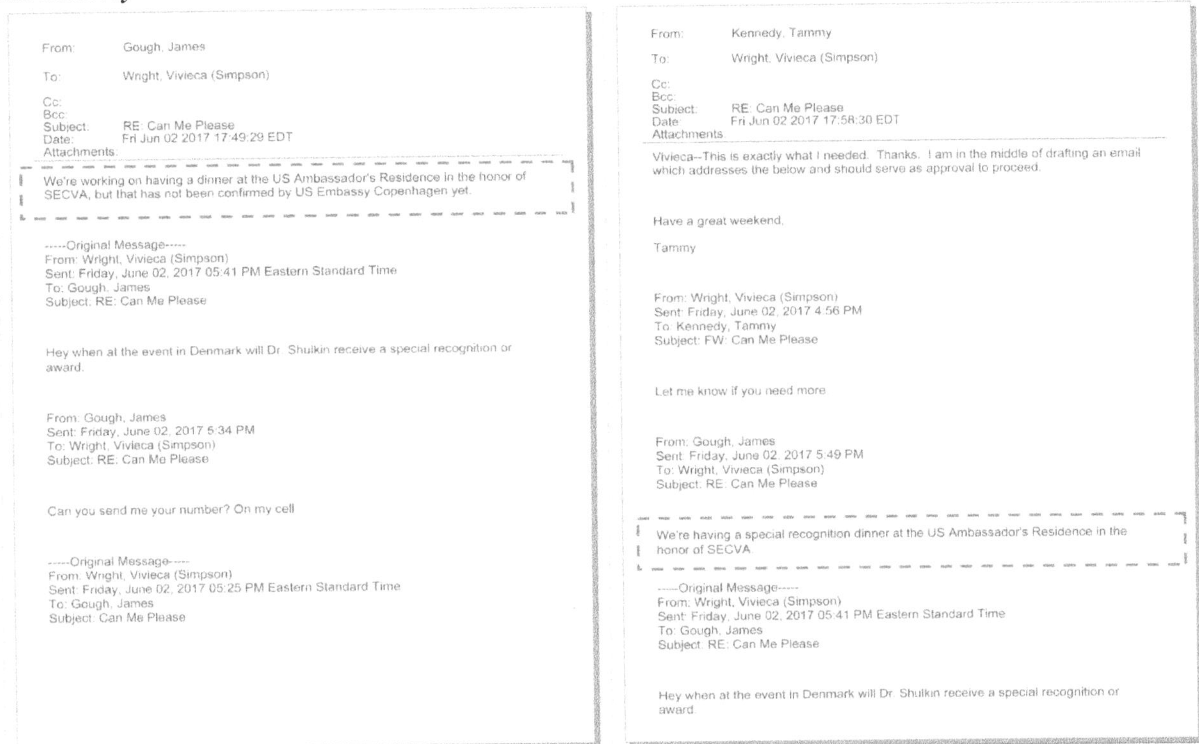

Figure 2. Dotted lines highlight the alteration in the email thread.

After her communications with Ms. Wright Simpson on June 2, Ms. Kennedy advised Ms. Wright Simpson via email that approval would be granted based on her understanding that Secretary Shulkin would be receiving an award. In an email sent a few moments later, Ms. Kennedy sought further clarification and confirmation from Ms. Wright Simpson:

---

[16] The 4:56 p.m. time stamp associated with the message "Let me know if you need more" appears out of sequence.

This is because this time stamp was recorded by the VA email system in Central Daylight-Saving Time.

Vivieca --Ask Mr. Gough to simply, succinctly set forth the nature of the special recognition please Vivieca. It is in fact an award, correct? In other words, it's not simply a reception, correct? For the VA's and Secretary's protection, I am just making sure that no issues are raised in the future.

After initially not responding and receiving a reminder from Ms. Kennedy, Ms. Wright Simpson replied six days later,

This is a diplomatic function and he is acting on behalf [of] the USA. Ministerial representatives from Canada, UK, New Zealand and Australia will be in attendance. We will be the biggest country there and instructing them on what we are doing. He will be sharing our best practices at their bequest [sic]. He is a keynote speaker on PSTD [sic]/MH, suicide and access to care for the VA. We are told he will get a special recognition, unfortunately I don't feel comfortable asking specifically if he is getting an award.[17]

Ms. Kennedy told OIG investigators that her approval of Dr. Bari's travel was based on Ms. Wright Simpson's communications and representations (made at least three times) that Secretary Shulkin was going to receive a special recognition or award.[19] OIG investigators showed Ms. Kennedy the original unaltered email that Mr. Gough sent to Ms. Wright Simpson as well as the email that Ms. Wright Simpson sent containing the altered text. Ms. Kennedy stated that based upon this new information, she would not have approved payment of Dr. Bari's travel.[18]

OIG investigators questioned Ms. Wright Simpson twice about the altered text in the email she forwarded to Ms. Kennedy. During her first interview, Ms. Wright Simpson initially claimed, "I don't recall whether I changed his email or not." After a short break, Ms. Wright Simpson requested to stop the interview so that she could consult with an attorney. OIG investigators stopped the interview. During the subsequent interview in which Ms. Wright Simpson was represented by counsel, she provided evasive responses to the question of whether she altered the email, repeating "I responded appropriately to the email." Other than her nonresponsive answers, Ms. Wright Simpson maintained that she did not recall whether she altered Mr. Gough's email prior to forwarding it to Ms. Kennedy.

---

[17] Ms. Wright Simpson's response to Ms. Kennedy relates to the Secretary's participation in the London Summit. There had never been a representation that Secretary Shulkin was going to get an award in London. Ms. Wright Simpson's earlier representations were that Secretary Shulkin was going to receive an award in Copenhagen. [19] The OIG found no evidence that Secretary Shulkin was aware of Ms. Wright Simpson's false representations or alteration of official records.

[18] Secretary Shulkin told OIG investigators that he did not receive an award during the Europe trip. At a luncheon hosted by the Danish Minister of Defense there was an exchange of what Secretary Shulkin described in his interview as "trinkets" that is typical between agencies. The Danish Minister gave a commemorative plaque, and Secretary Shulkin gave an engraved coin. Through counsel, Secretary Shulkin later took the position that the commemorative plaque (which he did not recall receiving during his interview with OIG investigators) was an award.

The OIG concluded that Ms. Wright Simpson willfully and knowingly made false representations to a VA ethics official and improperly altered an official record. Since Ms. Wright Simpson's false representations and alteration of an official record may have violated federal criminal statutes, the OIG referred this specific matter to the US Department of Justice (DOJ) to consider it for potential criminal prosecution; DOJ decided not to prosecute at this time.

Secretary Shulkin Improperly Accepted Wimbledon Tickets

Secretary Shulkin told OIG investigators that his wife is a "big tennis fan." When he learned that the Wimbledon tennis tournament would be taking place while they were scheduled to be in Europe, he attempted to get tickets. Secretary Shulkin said that he tried to get tickets through commercial websites and found there were no tickets available.[19] Secretary Shulkin stated that he obtained the tickets from Vicky Gosling, whom he had met professionally and described to OIG investigators as his wife's friend.

According to publicly available information, Victoria Gosling is a UK resident and the Head of Social Impact at Auden, a for-profit enterprise; a Military Director of Sage Foundation, the philanthropic affiliate of UK software company Sage Group plc;[20] and a Military Councilor for the Lawn Tennis Association, which is the national governing body for tennis in Great Britain, including Wimbledon. Ms. Gosling also served as CEO of the 2016 Invictus Games held in Orlando, Florida.[21] Secretary Shulkin stated that he and his wife met Ms. Gosling at an event at the British Embassy in Washington, D.C., in 2015. He and his wife also saw Ms. Gosling at two subsequent events—at the Invictus Games in Orlando, Florida in 2016 and at the Canadian Ambassador's home in Washington, D.C., on April 3, 2017. Six days after the April 3 event at the Canadian Ambassador's home, the president of a US-based nonprofit organization who was acquainted with Secretary Shulkin emailed him this inquiry: "Vicky

---

[19] Wimbledon tickets are famously difficult to obtain. See Luke Brown, "Wimbledon 2017: When does it start, how can I get tickets and how much will they cost?" *The Independent* July 6, 2017, available at: http://www.independent.co.uk/sport/tennis/wimbledon-2017-start-tickets-where-how-much-cost-price-buy-queueballot-live-qualifying-a7801801.html. Tickets are not made available for purchase by the general public until the day before the event.

[20] The Sage Group plc holds contracts with various federal agencies. The OIG has not identified a current contract between Sage Group and VA, although a small purchase ($1,147) of Sage software was made by VA in 2007, long before Secretary Shulkin's tenure. More recently, Sage Group (through the Sage Foundation) has sought support from VA officials for its philanthropic initiatives supporting veterans. For example, on May 3, 2017, the Sage Group plc publicized via Twitter a photo of then Acting VA Deputy Secretary Scott Blackburn and Ms. Gosling at a mental health event sponsored in part by the Sage Group. The tweet announced, "It was great to get Dept Secretary Scott

Blackburn's support for our Veteran Mentorship Programme." See also, "Sage Announces Global Program to Support Military Veterans Building Business Careers after Service." Sage plc Press Release. July 27, 2016, (describing "Sage Foundation's ambition to help more veterans build careers in business after military service," led by then Sage North American President, a U.S. Navy Veteran).

[21] The international Invictus games are "Prince Harry's sporting event for wounded, injured and sick Servicemen and women," https://invictusgamesfoundation.org.

Gosling who is on our steering committee for the Global Conference and the former CEO of INVICTUS, *asked to be introduced to you* [emphasis added]–are you fine with me connecting the two of you." Secretary Shulkin responded, "Glad to connect with Vicky." Other than the three official events described by Secretary Shulkin, the OIG found no evidence that Secretary Shulkin and Ms. Gosling met again until July 15 at Wimbledon.[22]

On June 24, 2017, Secretary Shulkin emailed the same acquaintance to request the current email address of Victoria Gosling.[23]

After receiving it, Secretary Shulkin sent an email to Ms. Gosling on June 25, 2017:

I will be traveling to London July 15-20 for a multi-national conference on veteran affairs- I don't know if you are planning on attending. I'll be with my wife and son so we hope to see some of the sights of London as well. Not knowing the city would you suggest certain things that we see? Also might you have any suggestions on how we might buy tickets to Wimbledon on the 15th?" Thank so much.

David Shulkin, MD
Secretary
US Department of Veterans Affairs

Ms. Gosling responded the same day,

Your email has just arrived at a perfect time as The Armed Forces Councilor I am able to purchase one pair of tickets for Wimbledon per day and I had purchased Ladies finals for my sister however she has literally just called to say she can no longer attend on 15th – so consider the pair of tickets yours.

Unfortunately the bad news is I am only able to purchase one pair (2 tickets) per day. I will try my best to get a 3rd…I can definitely get a ground pass to gain access to the grounds…I can definitely host all 3 of you in the Members Enclosure for lunch which is a fun thing to do (only Wimbledon membership is allowed – General public can't access) …Let me know if you want the tickets on 15th.

---

[22] The communication that Secretary Shulkin agreed to be introduced to Ms. Gosling appears inconsistent with statements that his wife was a friend and the tickets were unrelated to his official position, particularly when viewed in context with other indicators that no personal friendship existed with his wife as described later in this report. In a letter to Inspector General Missal dated February 11, 2018, counsel to Secretary Shulkin provided an affidavit from Ms. Gosling stating that she did not ask the mutual acquaintance for an introduction to Secretary Shulkin in April 2017. During the investigation, OIG investigators interviewed the acquaintance and asked about her email. She confirmed that Ms. Gosling did request that the acquaintance broker an introduction to Secretary Shulkin.

[23] In his interview with OIG investigators, Secretary Shulkin speculated that he may have had an outdated email address used by Ms. Gosling when she served as CEO of the Orlando Invictus games. As detailed later in this report, this was the same day that Dr. Bari asked Mr. Gough to try to obtain Wimbledon tickets.

Secretary Shulkin forwarded Ms. Gosling's email to his wife, and also responded to Ms. Gosling accepting the tickets for himself and Dr. Bari to the Ladies' Finals match, a grounds pass gaining entry to Wimbledon for his son, and an invitation for all three to attend lunch in the private members' enclosure as guests of Ms. Gosling.

Deleted Posting from Ms. Gosling's Twitter Account

Figure 3. Tweet and photo from Victoria Gosling on July 16, 2017, of Dr. Shulkin and his family.

Secretary Shulkin told OIG investigators that his acceptance of tickets to attend Wimbledon was not reviewed by VA ethics officials prior to the trip. He said that he did not ask VA ethics officials "to approve my personal attendances at events," and "[t]here is no separation between personal and business in the job that I have…this Wimbledon event had absolutely no business connection, whatsoever. It had personal reasons why we were going. I wouldn't think about clearing with ethics."[24] He stated that after learning of *The Washington Post's* "sensational story" about his Europe travel that he decided it would be "a good thing to disclose everything that I know about Vicky Gosling and the relationship and ask for ethics clearance."

On September 28, 2017, General Counsel Byrne wrote to DAEO Kennedy: "In an abundance of caution, I am asking you or someone on your team [to] conduct an expedited ethics review of [Secretary Shulkin's] acceptance of tickets to a sporting event in July in the United Kingdom? It is possible there is already an informal opinion in email traffic between your office and [Ms. Wright Simpson]. I have copied Secretary Shulkin on this email."

---

[24] Three months before Secretary Shulkin received the Wimbledon tickets, he was provided ethics training by VA's Senior Ethics Attorney that covered the rules relating to VA employees accepting gifts. As discussed later in this report, acceptance of the tickets was improper. The Senior Ethics Attorney told OIG investigators that although he could not specifically recall whether he so-advised Secretary Shulkin, it is his practice when presenting ethics training to "advise employees to contact [the Ethics Team] whenever they have any ethics questions about participation in official matters or outside activities."

At 5:02 p.m. EDT the same day, Ms. Kennedy emailed Mr. Byrne and Secretary Shulkin seeking additional information. Ms. Kennedy wrote:

I am following up on the following question regarding the Wimbledon tickets. Under 5 CFR 2635.204 (b) there is a gift exception which provides "An employee may accept a gift given under circumstances which make it clear that the gift is motivated by a family relationship or personal friendship rather than the position of the employee. Relevant factors in making such a determination include the history of the relationship and whether the family member or friend personally pays for the gift." Given this regulatory provision please advise:

1. Who is the friend? Where is he currently employed? What is his position?

2. How long have you known this friend?

3. Where did you initially meet this friend?

4. I am interested in questions that address that this person was more than a mere acquaintance or a business relationship. How often would you and this friend take trips or engage in non-business activities? What were these trips or non-business activities? Who was present at these trips/non-business activities? Would you and he often pay for functions/activities for one another?

5. Did this friend pay for this gift or did his company pay for these tickets?

6. If received from his business, under what circumstances did this friend receive the tickets? Were they given without reservation to your friend to use as he/she wished?

At 8:07 p.m. EDT Secretary Shulkin responded by paraphrasing and responding to some of Ms. Kennedy's questions, as follows:

Who is friend? —Vicky Golsing [*sic*]

Where is she employed—Vicky was the CEO [of the] Invictus Games in 2016 but has since left that position at the end of 2016. When we talked with her at Wimbledon she was not employed but was looking at a number of options. Her current title that she is using now is strategic advisor for the Invictus UK delegation- which I believe may be an unpaid position to help the team in preparing for the Toronto games.

How long have you known this friend?

My wife met Vicky first in October 2015 at the British ambassador residence and have been in touch since then several times. The next time they saw each other in person was at the Orlando Invictus games a little more than a year ago. My wife and she hit it off and have been in contact since and spent some time again on Vicky's visit to the US when she was here in March 2017. (its hard to get together more when living 5000 miles away). In April Merle told Vicky we were going to London and they made a plan to try to get together. There is no business relationship, but purely a social friendship between the two of them. We spent time at Wimbledon [*sic*] with Vicky and her husband. I believe he is active UK military. There was no discussion at all about business or any solicitation of any type.

How did you get the tickets?

We had contacted Vicky to get together knowing we were going to be in London. A week or so before we arrived Vicky told us that her sister had just told her that she was no longer going to be able to attend Wimbledon and her sister asked Vicky if she could use the tickets. Vicky know[s] Merle loves tennis and she invited us. We offered to pay but she insisted on taking us as friends.

Was there a business connection?

I am not aware of a business connection to these tickets and they were personal tickets of Vicky's sister - if there was any other source of these tickets Merle and I were not aware of it. We did not meet or speak to another other people at Wimbledon [*sic*] as this was purely a social time together.

Ms. Kennedy responded to Secretary Shulkin at 8:15 p.m. EDT and advised that based upon the information he provided, "the tickets fit within 5 CFR 2635.204, gift exception, where the gift is based on a personal relationship."

Through counsel, Secretary Shulkin also told OIG investigators that his wife and Ms. Gosling met at an official event in 2015 and "hit it off and remained in touch in the years since." The OIG requested that Secretary Shulkin produce any documents, emails, or any other information that would corroborate his characterization of the relationship between Dr. Bari and Ms. Gosling. Secretary Shulkin's counsel only produced a two-message text exchange dated September 28, 2017, in which Dr. Bari sought to reimburse Ms. Gosling for the Wimbledon tickets, but Ms. Gosling declined.[25] Secretary Shulkin produced no evidence that his wife and Ms. Gosling communicated with one another outside of official events prior their attendance together at Wimbledon in July 2017. The OIG reviewed Dr. Bari's telephone records and did not identify any calls between her and Ms. Gosling between July 2016 and February 1, 2018, other than calls on the afternoon of September 28, 2017, when Dr. Bari offered to pay for the Wimbledon tickets. The OIG also did not find any evidence that Dr. Bari and Ms. Gosling spent time together prior to Wimbledon, other than briefly at the three official group events in 2015, 2016, and 2017 where Dr. Bari accompanied Secretary Shulkin.

---

[25] This is the same day that General Counsel Byrne sought to obtain an ethics opinion on an expedited basis to support Secretary Shulkin's acceptance of the tickets.

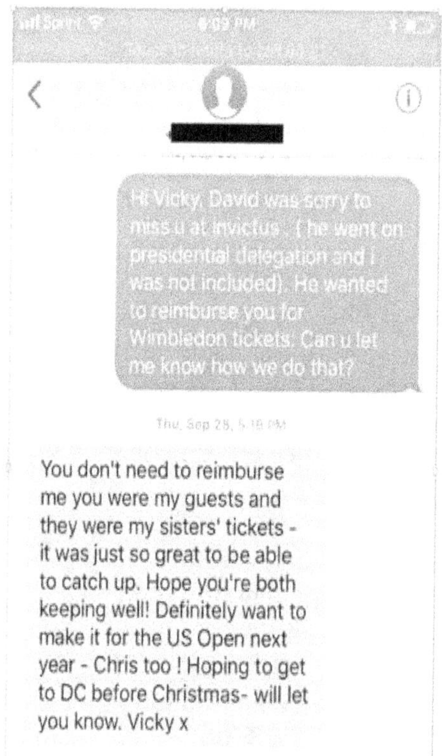

Figure 4. Text message exchange produced by Secretary Shulkin

Through counsel, Secretary Shulkin argues that the form and substance of this text exchange proves that Ms. Gosling and Dr. Bari were friends. With respect to the substance, OIG observes that the exchange is dated September 28, 2017, and therefore cannot be probative of the relationship as of June 25, 2017, when Secretary Shulkin accepted the Wimbledon tickets. Moreover, although Ms. Gosling's text message includes well-wishes (e.g., "Hope you're both keeping well!"), this content appears unusual when placed in its context: phone records reflect that at 4:29 p.m. EDT (less than an hour before this message was received), Dr. Bari and Ms. Gosling concluded an 11 minute 22 second phone call. This call commenced immediately after Ms. Gosling emailed Secretary Shulkin (4:17 p.m. EDT) to advise him that she had been contacted by a journalist regarding the Secretary's attendance at Wimbledon. Dr. Bari and Ms. Gosling conducted another call for approximately 17 minutes beginning at 6:47 p.m. EDT. With respect to form, Secretary Shulkin argues that Ms. Gosling's use of "x" as a closing is indicative of a close friendship. Cultural observers have described the frequent use of "x" as a Briticism that, when compared to similar American salutations, is distinguishable for its casual use and ubiquity.[26]

Ms. Kennedy based her conclusion that Secretary Shulkin's acceptance of the Wimbledon tickets was proper based on her understanding that the Secretary and his wife enjoyed a

---

[26] Eva Wiseman, "The joy of x in texts, tweets, and emails" *The Guardian*, January 27, 2013, https://www.theguardian.com/lifeandstyle/2013/jan/27/joy-x-texts-tweets-emails; Carrie Plitt, "X Please, We're British," *The Junket*, January 22, 2014, http://thejunket.org/2014/01/issue-ten/x-please-were-british/.

personal friendship with Ms. Gosling. OIG investigators provided Ms. Kennedy with additional information, including emails indicating that Ms. Gosling was seeking an introduction to Secretary Shulkin through an intermediary in April 2017. OIG investigators also provided Ms. Kennedy with email correspondence between Secretary Shulkin and Ms. Gosling on July 15 and 16, 2017 (starting hours after the tennis match), which revealed that Ms. Gosling requested Secretary Shulkin's assistance in gaining an invitation to the London Summit.[27] Based on this information, Ms. Kennedy revised her ethics opinion and stated that, "[Dr. Bari and Ms. Gosling were] not friends, as represented in [Secretary Shulkin's] response to me." She stated that the new information was "totally inconsistent with the information that [she] was provided."[28] OIG investigators also asked Ms. Gosling about the nature of her relationship with Secretary Shulkin and his wife.[29] Ms. Gosling summarized, I consider them to be friends. I like them. Do I see them regularly? No, I don't. . . Basically, due to the fact that I live over here, they live over there. If I lived over there, absolutely, I would spend more time with them, in answer to your question. But I don't. And, actually, I live a very, very busy life, as they do. So — but, when I go over there, and I was intending to go over there, but I haven't managed it yet, then I would be absolutely phoning them and letting them know that I was [in] the city and I would expect to go to dinner with them. But there you go. That's how I feel about them.

Ms. Gosling's statement appears to reflect genuine friendliness and good will toward Secretary Shulkin and Dr. Bari. Nonetheless, the objective facts as of the date the gift was made fail to satisfy the personal friendship exception to the prohibition against accepting gifts. Prior to arranging Wimbledon tickets, the interactions between Ms. Gosling, Dr. Shulkin, and Dr. Bari (however affable they may have been) were confined to three official business events, which Ms. Gosling confirmed during the interview. Additionally, during the course of the 26-minute interview, OIG investigators and Ms. Gosling referred to Dr. Bari only as Secretary Shulkin's "wife." Toward the end of the interview, OIG investigators asked whether Ms. Gosling could recall the first name of Secretary Shulkin's wife. After a long pause, Ms.

---

[27] Secretary Shulkin told OIG investigators that he did not "lift a finger" to assist Ms. Gosling. Ms. Gosling and Secretary Shulkin both told OIG investigators that she obtained an invitation from a source other than Secretary Shulkin. On July 18, 2017, an organizer of the London Summit wrote to Mr. Gough, "Secretary Shulkin may wish to be aware that Victoria Gosling will attend the conference on [Wednesday and Thursday] morning." Ms. Gosling told OIG investigators that, prior to the Wimbledon outing with Secretary Shulkin, she was already scheduled to attend the London Summit. Based on her communications with Secretary Shulkin in connection with Wimbledon, her statement to OIG investigators appears not to be accurate.

[28] The OIG presented the information to Ms. Kennedy prior to the OIG's unscheduled interview with Ms. Gosling on February 6, 2018. At the time of the OIG's discussion with Ms. Kennedy, Ms. Kennedy knew that the tickets were provided to Secretary Shulkin and his wife by Ms. Gosling, but she did not have confirmation that Ms. Gosling had paid for the tickets herself. This additional information, learned from the OIG's discussion with Ms. Gosling, does not change the OIG's conclusion that the friendship exception is inapplicable. The balance of the information provided by Ms. Gosling during her interview was consistent with the facts that were considered in the OIG's and Ms. Kennedy's analysis.

[29] The OIG's interview of Ms. Gosling was conducted on an unscheduled basis on February 6, 2018. OIG investigators identified themselves to Ms. Gosling at the outset of the call and asked if they could interview her. She agreed voluntarily.

Gosling stated, "You actually -- I think that kept throwing me. I'm actually having a genuine blank here." She was unable to recall Dr. Bari's name before the interview concluded.

The OIG's conclusion that neither Secretary Shulkin nor Dr. Bari had a personal friendship with Ms. Gosling, as defined by 5 CFR 2635.204, is also supported by an example accompanying the rule, which clarifies the personal friendship exception. In that example, a government employee meets an individual at an official meeting. Thereafter, they granted each other access to their social media networks and communicated occasionally. Under this scenario, the government employee would not be able to take advantage of the personal friendship exception because "they did not communicate further in their personal capacities, carry on extensive personal interactions, or meet socially outside of work." As noted, there is no evidence that Secretary Shulkin or Dr. Bari and Ms. Gosling interacted outside of three official functions before the gift of the Wimbledon tickets. Therefore, this example supports that the relationship did not meet the personal friendship exception.

An advisory opinion from the Office of Government Ethics explores the circumstance applicable here, where a relationship develops exclusively in connection with official duties:

Where a personal relationship develops from an on-going work relationship, it can be very difficult to clearly establish that the gift is not being given because of the employee's official position. A gift given out of appreciation for some action the employee took, particularly one that relates to an employee's official responsibilities, is not clearly motivated by a personal relationship. Therefore, an employee bears a considerable burden in establishing that a gift is based on a personal relationship rather than the employee's Government position. This burden may be exacerbated even further by testamentary gifts where gifts to non-family members may be considered suspect.

One must look to the circumstances surrounding the gift when a personal relationship is at issue. Factors indicating a personal relationship include the length of time of the relationship, the intimacy of the relationship including any family interaction, the nature of personal activities outside the work context, and the frequency of outside contacts.[30]

In an email response to the OIG's repeated requests for an interview, Ms. Gosling wrote that "[Secretary Shulkin] and his wife are friends of mine." As noted earlier, she further stated that she offered the tickets to Secretary Shulkin and his family "to thank them for their personal support to me whilst I was CEO Invictus Games Orlando."[31] Ms. Gosling clarified this statement when she spoke with OIG investigators,

---

[30] Advisory Opinion, Office of Government Ethics, *Letter to a Law Firm*, March 21, 2006 at 2, https://www.oge.gov/Web/OGE.nsf/All%20Advisories/C72D3145E59B78BF85257E96005FBE03/$FILE/7be85d5345874af8aaf23f452e5aa7954.pdf?open.

[31] The OIG first sought to interview Ms. Gosling on a voluntary basis via an email request on December 15, 2017. Investigators made at least 19 additional attempts to contact her on December 18, 20, 21, and January 9, 23, and 24, using various methods, including email, text, phone, and courier. The OIG received an email from

Investigator: Now you had mentioned that, um, providing Dr. Shulkin with the tickets was your way to thank him for his support. What did he do exactly to support you for the Invictus Games?

Ms. Gosling: — Look, I had the tickets. I enjoy his company. I enjoy his wife's company. It wasn't just about thanking him for helping me with support because, actually, I had a, a lot of gratitude for the way that the U.S. in general supported me when I brought the games across. Not just him specifically. I really got on very well with his wife …

Federal ethics rules prohibit the solicitation or acceptance of any gift given because of the employee's official position, unless an exception applies.[32] In this situation, the OIG concludes that Ms. Gosling gave a gift of the Wimbledon tickets because of Secretary Shulkin's official position.[33] Ms. Gosling admits that the tickets were given, in part, to thank Secretary Shulkin, Dr. Bari, and the "U.S. in general" for support in connection with the Orlando Invictus Games.[34] Secretary Shulkin's acceptance of the tickets was contrary to 5 CFR§ 2635.202(b), which prohibits him from accepting gifts based upon his official position. Prior to Wimbledon, there was no evidence that Secretary Shulkin or his wife met with Ms. Gosling at an event other than the three gatherings he attended in his official capacity.

In addition, by virtue of her business relationships (whether for profit or not), Ms. Gosling may also meet the definition of a "prohibited source," which would be another basis for the gift of the Wimbledon tickets to be improper.[35] The OIG was unable to fully explore this topic with Ms. Gosling because she did not timely respond to repeated requests to schedule an

---

Ms. Gosling on January 30, 2018, stating that she was willing to speak with OIG investigators voluntarily. In that email, she agreed to talk with OIG investigators, but she did not thereafter respond to the OIG's efforts to schedule an interview. OIG investigators then contacted her by telephone on February 6, 2018 and conducted an unscheduled interview with her consent.

[32] 5 C.F.R. § 2635.202.

[33] Secretary Shulkin accepted the tickets without knowing what Ms. Gosling paid for them (though he did inquire via email at the time, "Just let me know how much I owe you"). Ms. Gosling told OIG investigators that she paid for the tickets with her own funds and that she obtained the tickets at a discount. She was unable to recall the cost of the tickets. Secretary Shulkin stated that the combined market value of the tickets and grounds pass was £344 (approximately $450). The market value of the tickets and grounds pass is "deemed to be the face value" of the tickets and grounds pass. 5 C.F.R. § 2635.203.

[34] At least one federal court has interpreted the phrase "circumstances 'make it clear' that the motivation is personal" from 5 C.F.R. § 2635.204(b) to mean that the "personal friendship exception is only applicable if the gift is based 'solely' on a personal relationship" and that it would be improper for a federal employee to accept a gift given "at least in part on doing business." *Baltimore v. Clinton*, 900 F. Supp. 2d 21, 29 (D.D.C. 2012). Here, the OIG concludes that the circumstances of the gift do not "make it clear" that the motivation was personal.

[35] 5 C.F.R. § 2635.203 states, "Prohibited source means any person who: (1) Is seeking official action by the employee's agency; (2) Does business or seeks to do business with the employee's agency; (3) Conducts activities regulated by the employee's agency; (4) Has interests that may be substantially affected by the performance or nonperformance of the employee's official duties; or (5) Is an organization a majority of whose members are described in paragraphs (d)(1) through (4) of this section."

---

interview.[36] However, Ms. Gosling's status as a prohibited source is supported by her association with the Invictus Games, an important veterans charitable cause that has accepted support from VA.[37] In addition, on July 15, 2017, in connection with soliciting an invitation to the London Summit, Ms. Gosling wrote to Secretary Shulkin and revealed specific business interests that she was pursuing,

2 days of programme looks great particularly with regards to some of the work I'm doing with Invictus Games, the Global Mental Health Strategy, and the corporate work with the Career Transition Partnership, and the Business in the Community work, along with helping veterans transition through the mentoring programme - I would love to be able to attend the lectures if at all possible just to listen to the latest thoughts in this space.[38]

I am seeing CDS today (Air Marshal) so I'm happy to ████████ I can attend, failing that I wonder if there's anything you can do so that I can attend in a US/UK relationship capacity having done so much work with the VA and previous administration for Orlando when bringing the Invictus Games to USA as the CEO?

It is never permissible to accept a gift given on the basis of an employee's official position. However, an employee may accept gift if the circumstances make it clear that the gift was motivated by personal friendship and not the employee's official position. Similarly, a gift given by a prohibited source may be legally accepted if it falls under an exception to the ethics rules, such as a gift received from someone with whom the employee has a personal friendship. However, as discussed above, neither the VA DAEO nor the OIG believes that there was a personal friendship between Dr. Bari and Ms. Gosling as defined in the rules. The OIG does not find that any other exception to the prohibition against accepting a gift is relevant in this situation. Finally, even if the personal friendship exception did apply in this instance, making the gift permissible, Secretary Shulkin should have considered declining the gift on the basis of federal ethics standards, which he did not do.[39] The Standards of Ethical Conduct for Employees of the Executive Branch admonishes employees to "consider declining otherwise permissible gifts if they believe that a reasonable person with knowledge of the relevant facts would question the employee's integrity or impartiality as a result of

---

[36] When OIG investigators reached Ms. Gosling, she agreed to do the interview and told investigators near the end of questioning that she was in her car. The interview lasted for 26 minutes, which was insufficient to explore all relevant topics.

[37] In 2016, VA provided onsite medical care to athletes competing in the Invictus Games Orlando. VA Office of Public Affairs, "Hundreds of injured military Veterans from around the globe to compete in the 2016 Invictus Games: VA to provide onsite medical and mental health support to international athletes in Orlando," news release, May 6, 2016, https://www.va.gov/opa/pressrel/includes/viewPDF.cfm?id=2786.

[38] Ms. Gosling's email responds to a message sent by Secretary Shulkin during the evening of July 15, 2017 (after the Wimbledon match), in which he forwarded a copy of the London Summit agenda.

[39] Although Secretary Shulkin did offer to repay Ms. Gosling for the tickets, there is no suggestion that this was motivated by a decision to decline a gift on ethical grounds, nor did Secretary Shulkin insist on that basis. Secretary Shulkin told OIG investigators that he did not clear the gift with ethics, and that but for the media inquiry on September 28, 2017, he would not have done so.

accepting the gift."[40] When making this determination, employees "may consider, among other relevant factors, whether: (i) The gift has a high market value; (ii) The timing of the gift creates the appearance that the donor is seeking to influence an official action; (iii) The gift was provided by a person who has interests that may be substantially affected by the performance or nonperformance of the employee's official duties; and (iv) Acceptance of the gift would provide the donor with significantly disproportionate access."[41] VA policy states that "if after taking these factors into consideration the employee believes that a reasonable person would question the employee's integrity or impartiality or the integrity or partiality of VA programs or operations, then the employee should not accept the gift."[42] Through counsel, Secretary Shulkin stated that the decision whether a "legally permissible gift should be accepted is the employee's to make," not the OIG's.[43] The OIG agrees. Here, however, the gift was not legally permissible. Nonetheless, to the extent that Secretary Shulkin believed that the gift was legally permissible, VA policy obligated him to consider declining the gift. Relevant factors in such an evaluation included the reasonable person's perspective concerning the value of the tickets; the circumstances of the relationship with Ms. Gosling, including her requests for access to an international summit of veterans' affairs ministers; Ms. Gosling's association with charities and businesses that have relationships with VA; and other facts discussed throughout this report. Thus, based on Ms. Kennedy's revised opinion and the OIG's independent analysis, the gift of Wimbledon tickets, any food, and anything else of value provided to Secretary Shulkin and his family by Ms. Gosling that day was an improper gift given on the basis of his official position.

Secretary Shulkin Directed the Misuse of a Subordinate's Official Time

Mr. Gough told OIG investigators that Secretary Shulkin directed him to coordinate with his wife to schedule the tourist activities that they wanted to do on nonofficial time. Secretary Shulkin corroborated this account to OIG investigators, stating, "I didn't have any interest in doing this. I basically didn't care what we did in our off time, and so I said, you deal with my wife." [44] In an email to a colleague referencing this topic, Mr. Gough wrote, "Boss told me 'if

---

[40] 5 C.F.R. § 2635.201(b)(1); VA policy implementing this rule states that employees "*must* make a preliminary determination of whether the employee should accept the gift." (Emphasis added.) VA Designated Agency Ethics Official memorandum, February 23, 2017. (See Appendix A.)

[41] 5 C.F.R. § 2635.201(b)(2); VA policy implementing this rule states that employees "must consider" the four factors. VA Designated Agency Ethics Official memorandum, February 23, 2017. (See Appendix A.)

[42] VA Designated Agency Ethics Official memorandum, February 23, 2017. (See Appendix A.) Secretary Shulkin received in-person ethics training in his office one-on-one with a VA ethics official on March 20, 2017.

[43] Secretary Shulkin argues that this analysis is nonbinding and hortatory. Indeed, 5 C.F.R. § 2635.201 uses permissive language and there is no penalty for accepting a legally permissible gift. However, Secretary Shulkin is also subject to VA policy implementing this rule, which is more insistent in that it requires employees to preliminarily consider declining a permissible gift. VA Designated Agency Ethics Official memorandum, February 23, 2017. (See Appendix A.)

[44] Through counsel, Secretary Shulkin stated that on June 23, 2017 "Mr. Gough on his own initiative undertook the detailed planning of tourist activities. Only when Mr. Gough approached the Secretary with this information did the Secretary refer Mr. Gough to Dr. Bari." Irrespective of any self-initiated improper use of official time by

---

she's happy, I'm happy and you're happy.' Mr. Gough told OIG investigators that Dr. Bari had "a lot of different suggestions" for tourist activities and that he was responsible for accommodating her requests.

Mr. Gough stated that his involvement in the planning was necessary in order to coordinate security coverage for Secretary Shulkin. However, emails reveal that Mr. Gough was serving as a *de facto* personal travel concierge to the Secretary and his wife by providing detailed tourist planning and travel research services on official time at Secretary Shulkin's direction. Mr. Gough's tourist planning activities were in excess of what was reasonably necessary to perform any official security planning duties. For example, on June 23, 2017, the day before Secretary Shulkin obtained the Wimbledon tickets from Ms. Gosling, Dr. Bari wrote to Mr. Gough, forwarding a series of restaurant and activity recommendations and further inquiring, "Is there earlier flight from Copenhagen? Wimbledon tickets? High tea? Roman baths in [B]ath. Would want to do baths not just tour."

In an email on June 24, Dr. Bari wrote to Mr. Gough:

Sites to cover, we can go in any order u think works but we like to be busy, we often don't spend too much time at palaces or cathedrals. Secretary agrees that need some time to check in with work answer emails or call back each weekday so can be flexible in later afternoon after we do sightseeing.

Dr. Bari's list of sites and activities to cover included Buckingham Palace, Westminster Abbey, the Churchill War Rooms, a Thames River cruise, London Eye, Tower Bridge, Tower of London (including the Ceremony of the Keys), Shakespeare's Globe, Trafalgar Square, Piccadilly Circus, St. Paul's Cathedral, Hyde Park, Kensington Palace, and Harrods. She also added events to consider, including Wimbledon, theatre tickets, day trips (to Stonehenge, Windsor, Bath), and high tea. She concluded her email with, "Thanks, I sent restaurants secretary liked under separate pdf."

Although Secretary Shulkin ultimately obtained tickets to the July 15 Wimbledon Ladies' Final, Dr. Bari had also asked Mr. Gough about obtaining tickets to Wimbledon. Mr. Gough advised Dr. Bari on June 29 that he was attempting to use diplomatic connections to arrange Wimbledon tickets to the Gentlemen's Final for the Secretary and his wife:

I'm asking ppl from the Embassy and the UK government about Wimbledon tickets and have not had much luck. There are still a couple more people who have to get back to me, but this is what I'm looking at price-wise now just on stubhub. [Mr. Gough's email included a now-expired link to tickets on Stubhub.com for the Sunday, July 16, 2017, Gentlemen's Final at Wimbledon.]

Mr. Gough, Secretary Shulkin ignores his own stewardship obligations. "An employee shall not encourage, direct, coerce, or request a subordinate to use official time to perform activities other than those required in the performance of official duties or authorized in accordance with law or regulation." 5 C.F.R. § 2635.705.

On Friday, June 30, Mr. Gough sent another email responding to Dr. Bari's inquiries, proposing an itinerary for a day trip that included stops in the UK towns of Windsor and Bath:

Dr. Bari – are you free for a call? This is what the Sunday trip would look like to Windsor and Bath. If you're good with this, please let me know so that I can send this day to all the security teams for them to get to work on…Everything from Trip Advisor to the actual website has the Roman Baths being ruins, and you aren't able to get in them. It's more of like walking through ruins. I've tried looking around the town of Bath to see if there is a spa that would allow you to do this but haven't been successful. Is there something you found that I didn't?

Dr. Bari responded, "Call me later but i dont think this will work[.]" Mr. Gough forwarded this email exchange to another staff member and expressed frustration with the many requests he had been receiving from Dr. Bari. He wrote, "I would have been finished with this a week ago…." In an email the next day, he told the staff member, "Copenhagen is good to go. Dr. Bari changed a lot of stuff for London, so I'm re-doing a lot of the unofficial stuff today." The emails support that his planning efforts were not merely incident to the planning of the Secretary's security detail. Mr. Gough could have appropriately conveyed to the security teams the requisite details pertaining to the Secretary's leisure time activities without engaging in the extensive research and planning tasks.

Personal activities for the Denmark trip included touring Amalienborg Palace for the Changing of the Guard; visiting Christiansborg Palace, Rosenborg Castle, and Frederiksborg Castle; taking a boat tour of Copenhagen from Nyhavn Canal; and shopping in Copenhagen. There was also an unplanned excursion across the border to Malmo, Sweden, for dinner on their last day, July 14.

Mr. Gough had official "Trip Book" itineraries printed at government expense for the Secretary and the official party at a cost of $100 each (15 copies). The Trip Book included the following scheduled visits to tourist sites and activities in London: Wimbledon, Thames River Cruise, Trafalgar Square, Churchill War Room, St. James's Park, Buckingham Palace, Hyde Park, and Kensington Palace, Westminster Abbey, Piccadilly Circus, St. Paul's Cathedral, Tower of London, Tower Bridge, Shakespeare's Globe, London Eye, and Windsor Castle. The itinerary section of the Trip Book is included as Appendix B.

The OIG Cannot Determine the "Essential" Nature of the Travel in Keeping with the Secretary's Memorandum

On June 29, 2017, less than two weeks before the start of the Europe trip, Secretary Shulkin issued a memorandum titled, *Essential Employee Travel*, which required senior VA leaders to determine whether employee travel in their organization was essential. The stated purpose of this memorandum was to generate savings through decreased employee travel. The OIG cannot determine whether the value of the trip to VA, including the value provided by each participant in the trip, was consistent with the Secretary's memorandum."[45]

The OIG Did Not Fully Assess the Costs to VA

The total cost for the VA delegation to travel to Europe in July 2017 was at least $122,334, including $100,987 in traveler-incurred expenses and $21,347 in reimbursements to the US Embassies in London and Copenhagen.[48] A breakdown of costs follows:

Total Traveler Reimbursements	Description
$42,230	Airfare and associated travel agent fees[49]
$33,888	Lodging per *diem*
$15,947	Meals and Incidentals per diem
$9,635	Miscellaneous costs, such as airport parking, airline seat upgrades, checked baggage fees, gratuities, and laundry

US Embassy Reimbursements $12,062	Description
$9,285[50]	US Embassy, London, UK for travel support including vehicles, chauffeur services, tolls, and parking
	US Embassy, Copenhagen, Denmark for travel support including private wireless internet, driver overtime, vehicles, and baggage transport

Federal travel regulations and VA policy permit employees traveling on official duty to combine official travel with personal travel under appropriate circumstances. When an employee elects to combine them, including travel by an indirect route for personal convenience, the employee is responsible for paying any additional cost.[51] VA requires travelers to provide a Travel Cost Comparison Worksheet, which compares the actual cost of the trip with and without personal travel expenses. Properly prepared travel authorizations help VA and travelers determine when to charge for annual leave, when to Shulkin, Dr.

---

[45] The composition of the VA Delegation meant that three of VA's most senior leaders were out of the country together for an extended period. While in Copenhagen, Secretary Shulkin was informed that *The Boston Globe* was planning to publish a story detailing allegations of substandard care at the Manchester VA Medical Center. Secretary

Alaigh, and Ms. Wright Simpson were in contact with VA officials in Washington and decided that they could manage this crisis from Europe in an effective manner.

48   OIG investigators have not analyzed indirect costs, such as staffing, overtime, and other costs not recorded in the travel voucher system or as part of the interagency agreements detailed here.

49   The OIG analysis revealed that the initial cost of the airfare for all passengers was $25,478. The $15,699 increase occurred due to itinerary changes made by some travelers. The largest increase was associated with Secretary Shulkin's medical need to upgrade his return trip from London to business class. This added $10,355 to the air transportation costs ($5,177 each for Secretary Shulkin and his accompanying security detail member).

50   The OIG did not have access to final cost information from the US Embassy in Denmark. This amount reflects an estimate generated by VA travel planning personnel on June 26, 2017.

51   41 CFR §§ 301-2.2, 301-2.3, 301-2.4, 301-11.21 and VA Travel Administration, Volume XIV, Chapter 1, Appendix D (May 2013); see also Appendix A. reimburse travel expenses, and who is financially responsible if a traveler becomes ill or is injured while away from the office.

On December 7, 2017, a travel coordinator involved in the Europe trip planning told OIG investigators that no cost comparisons were prepared.[46] Although the full extent cannot be determined without further auditing by VA, the OIG determined that arrangements made in consideration of personal conveniences did impact the cost of the travel. For example, on June 26, 2017, VA travel staff changed the itineraries of Secretary Shulkin, his wife, and five other members of the VA delegation to depart on an earlier flight from Copenhagen to London in order to accommodate the personal excursion by Secretary Shulkin and Dr. Bari to the Ladies' Final tennis match at Wimbledon. This change resulted in $372 in travel agency transaction fees.[47] This change also added $1,733 to lodging costs because VA paid for an early hotel check-in for six rooms, including for Secretary Shulkin and Ms. Wright Simpson.[48]

In another example of insufficient documentation, Ms. Wright Simpson's original roundtrip economy class airfare was issued on June 16, 2017, at a cost of $1,101. On June 22, 2017, her ticket was modified and the new economy class airfare cost $4,041. The dates of the travel remained the same, but the intermediate connection point changed from a 210-minute

---

[46] Secretary Shulkin relies on staff to make travel arrangements and to document approvals and other requirements.

[47] VA incurs transaction fees from its travel agent every time a booking is made or changed. Travel records reflect numerous other itinerary changes, totaling $3,492 for all participants.

[48] The itinerary reflects a planned arrival at the London hotel between 9:30 and 10:30 a.m. local time. In order to accommodate early occupancy at the London hotel, VA paid for two hotel rooms for each of these six travelers on the night of June 14, 2017—one in Copenhagen (where the delegation spent the night) and the other in London (to ensure immediate access to rooms the following morning upon arrival).

connection in London to a 320-minute connection in New York. Travel records are insufficient to determine what justification, if any, was provided for this substantially higher-priced routing.

The OIG identified other insufficiently documented circumstances, which require further analysis and validation by VA. For example, when a traveler's meals are otherwise furnished (such as meals included as part of a conference), federal employees must reduce the corresponding meal *per diem* claimed. Travel records indicate that some, but not all, meeting attendees reduced their meal *per diem* claims to account for meals furnished during meetings. Documentation was insufficient to determine whether an appropriate basis existed for those attendees who did not reduce their *per diem* meal claims. In addition, to the extent that any of the travelers combined personal travel with official travel, VA payment for lodging, meals, and incidentals would not be appropriate during periods of personal travel.

The OIG observed other irregularities, including potential exchange rate errors, double reimbursement of room taxes that were itemized and also included in the room rate, and one security personnel's expense voucher that included an inexplicable $3,825 overpayment for airport parking and $2,718 overpayment for lodging.

Inadequate documentation makes it impossible for the OIG to determine precisely which costs, if any, should have been borne by the traveler, rather than the government. In addition, the OIG did not review time and attendance records of participants.

VA Made Misleading Statements to the Media

VA's Assistant Secretary for Public and Intergovernmental Affairs John Ullyot told OIG investigators that on September 27, 2017, he first learned that *The Washington Post* was working on the previously mentioned news story concerning Secretary Shulkin's July 2017 travel to Europe. The next afternoon, General Counsel Byrne directed his ethics personnel to "conduct an expedited ethics review of [Secretary Shulkin's] acceptance of tickets to a sporting event in July in the United Kingdom."[49]

On September 29, 2017, *The Washington Post* reported that according to an emailed statement from VA press secretary Curt Cashour, "All of Shulkin's activities on the Europe trip, including his attendance at Wimbledon, 'were reviewed and approved by ethics counsel.'"

Senior Ethics official Jonathan Gurland told OIG investigators that he had "a bit of a visceral reaction" to *The Washington Post* article, and Ms. Kennedy said the statement reflected negatively on them professionally. Ms. Kennedy and Mr. Gurland both told OIG investigators that, after reading the article, they contacted General Counsel Byrne to protest the portion of

---

[49] Mr. Byrne's request is time stamped 1:23 p.m. EDT. Counsel for Secretary Shulkin provided the OIG with a text message from Ms. Gosling to Dr. Bari at 5:16 p.m. EDT, declining to accept Dr. Bari's offer of reimbursement made earlier that day. That was the same text message exchange submitted to the OIG as the only evidence of the personal friendship between Ms. Gosling and Dr. Bari over the previous years.

the statement that read, "All activities including Wimbledon were reviewed and approved by ethics counsel." Mr. Gurland explained to OIG investigators that prior to the Secretary's travel, VA ethics counsel had only "advised on the one narrow issue" of whether VA could pay for Dr. Bari's travel expenses. In Mr. Gurland and Ms. Kennedy's view, ethics counsel did not approve the acceptance of Wimbledon tickets in advance, nor were they ever asked to review or approve "all activities" associated with the Secretary's July 2017 Europe trip.

Mr. Ullyot told OIG investigators that he drafted the September 29 statement using details provided by Secretary Shulkin. He said that Secretary Shulkin dictated portions of the statement, including the phrase "all activities including Wimbledon were reviewed and approved by Ethics Counsel." Mr. Ullyot provided a hard copy draft statement to

Mr. Byrne for review and approval. Mr. Byrne stated that he "may have edited some of it, [but] not much because I only look[ed] at this thing for about 20 seconds" prior to giving it "a green light" for release. Neither Mr. Ullyot nor Mr. Byrne could recall whether Mr. Byrne actually suggested any revisions to the statement prior to its approval for release.

Secretary Shulkin told OIG investigators that he had "no idea" where that statement originated, and that he did not "deal with the media." In addition, he said, "I generally don't write statements for the VA press secretary…I don't recall ever sitting there and saying to the press secretary, here is what you should say." He said, "Maybe they showed it to me. I don't know." Mr. Ullyot stated that he did not confirm the accuracy of the statement with VA ethics attorneys involved in the review and approval of the Secretary's activities, but instead consulted only Mr. Byrne.

Mr. Byrne told OIG investigators his ethics team was "upset about the optics, like ethics approved the optics of using taxpayer money to go [to] Europe." He clarified that in his view, the intent behind the statement was to convey that the ethics counsel had "looked at the components of the trip that were reviewable by ethics." Mr. Byrne acknowledged that it may have been better if the statement read, "all activities requiring an ethics review were reviewed," rather than "all activities including Wimbledon were reviewed and approved by ethics counsel." However, Mr. Byrne stated that he was rushed in his review of the statement before it was released. VA did not issue any subsequent statements to clarify the nature, timing, or extent of the ethics review referenced in the September 29 statement.

In a video interview with a *Washington Post* reporter on November 9, 2017, covering a number of issues, Secretary Shulkin addressed questions about his attendance at Wimbledon.

Secretary Shulkin: Well, this is your chance. Ask me any question you want.

Reporter: Well, all right. The Wimbledon tickets [Secretary Shulkin interjects, "Yes?"], did you buy those?

Secretary Shulkin: Yes, they were privately done, no government money.

Reporter: Okay. So they weren't given to you as a gift by folks at the Invictus Games or anything like that?

Secretary Shulkin: No, we went with friends. There was no business connection to that and there was no government money and it was on a Saturday for one match and last time I heard . . . there's nothing illegal about going to enjoy a sporting event.[50]

Secretary Shulkin did not disclose to the reporter that the tickets were a gift from the former CEO of the Invictus Games, who was still affiliated with Invictus in another capacity when they met at Wimbledon. Secretary Shulkin explained to OIG investigators that his response "yes" was an acknowledgement to the reporter that he wished to address the question about the Wimbledon tickets, and that he was not responding to the substance of the reporter's question ("Did you buy those?") when he said "yes." The OIG determined that Secretary Shulkin said "yes" twice in this portion of the reporter's interview.[51] The first instance is consistent with Secretary Shulkin's explanation.

The OIG concluded that VA's statement to *The Washington Post* on September 29, 2017, was misleading because it stated that ethics counsel had reviewed "all activities" associated with the Europe trip, which was not accurate. The OIG determined that VA's release of the misleading statement was caused, in part, by ineffective legal review of the statement by Mr. Byrne. Secretary Shulkin compounded the misconceptions caused by VA's statement by stating that he paid for the tickets and they were not given by someone affiliated with the Invictus Games.

Conclusion

Although the OIG does not assess the value VA gained from the Secretary and his delegation's three-and-a-half days of meetings in Copenhagen and London at a cost of at least $122,334, the investigation revealed serious derelictions by VA personnel concerning the Europe trip. There were five key findings related to poor judgment and/or misconduct:

First, VA Chief of Staff Wright Simpson made false statements and altered a document so that the trip expenses for Dr. Bari would be paid for by VA. The OIG referred this conduct to the US Department of Justice (DOJ) for its consideration; DOJ decided not to pursue criminal prosecution at this time.

Second, Secretary Shulkin improperly accepted a gift of two tickets and a grounds pass to the Ladies' Final tennis match at Wimbledon on July 15, 2017. When the OIG provided ethics counsel with additional information, she determined that the tickets should not have been

---

[50] The OIG agrees that depending on the facts and circumstances, it may not be necessary to seek ethics review for attendance at routine and/or low-cost sporting events with friends. As discussed throughout, the OIG concluded that the relationship between Ms. Gosling and Dr. Bari and Secretary Shulkin did not satisfy the personal friendship exception provided by 5 C.F.R. § 2635.204(b).

[51] The full interview is available for viewing at http://wapo.st/2ztOoyC.

accepted as a gift. The OIG separately made the same determination with the benefit of even more information adduced in its investigation.

Third, Secretary Shulkin directed a subordinate to devote the use of official time to provide personal travel planning assistance to Secretary Shulkin and Dr. Bari in connection with the nonofficial components of the trip. The personal assistance was extensive and went beyond what was needed to inform security personnel of their movements.

Fourth, VA's documentation was inadequate to allow the OIG to assess the accuracy and appropriateness of the costs to VA for the trip, but the investigators' analysis revealed discrepancies and potential errors that warrant a closer examination by VA auditors.

Finally, in response to press attention regarding Secretary Shulkin's Europe travel, VA issued an inaccurate statement to the press that "all activities" of the Europe trip were reviewed by ethics counsel. Moreover, in an interview with *The Washington Post,* Secretary Shulkin incorrectly stated that he purchased the Wimbledon tickets and they were not a gift from anyone associated with the Invictus Games.

Recommendations

Recommendation 1: Secretary Shulkin reimburses the $4,312 paid by VA to cover Dr. Bari's travel costs.[52]

Recommendation 2: Secretary Shulkin consults with the Office of General Counsel to determine the value of the Wimbledon tickets; grounds pass; and any food, parking, and other tangible benefits Ms. Gosling provided in connection with Wimbledon and reimburse that amount to her. If Ms. Gosling declines to accept reimbursement, Secretary Shulkin reimburses such amount to the US Treasury.

Recommendation 3: The Deputy Secretary of Veterans Affairs confers with the Offices of General Counsel, Human Resources, and Accountability and Whistleblower Protection to determine the appropriate administrative action to take, if any, against Ms. Wright Simpson and any other individuals associated with the Europe trip.

Recommendation 4: The Deputy Secretary of Veterans Affairs ensures that a thorough audit is conducted of the expense vouchers, travel authorizations, and the time and attendance records for all travelers on the Europe trip. Any overpayments should be reimbursed to VA by the traveler and any required leave adjustments should be made. Detailed results of the audits, including supporting documentation, shall be provided to the Office of Inspector General no later than thirty days following the publication of this report.

Recommendation 5: The Deputy Secretary of Veterans Affairs ensures that the Office of General Counsel (i) reviews and enhances the training provided to staff on travel planning, approvals, and the solicitation or acceptance of gifts; and (ii) provides refresher training on these topics to all travelers on the Europe trip as well as all staff involved in the planning and implementation of the trip.

---

[52] Additional reimbursements may be required as identified by the audit in Recommendation 4.

Appendix A

Relevant Laws, Regulations, Standards of Conduct, and VA Policy

False **Statements**

18 USC § 1001 – Makes it a felony for anyone, in any matter within the jurisdiction of the federal government, who

knowingly and willfully falsifies, conceals, or covers up by any trick, scheme, or device a material fact; makes any materially false, fictitious, or fraudulent statement or representation; or makes or uses any false writing or document knowing the same to contain any materially false, fictitious, or fraudulent statement or entry.

5 CFR § 735.203 – Prohibits federal government employees from engaging in criminal, infamous, dishonest, immoral, or notoriously disgraceful conduct, or other conduct prejudicial to the Government.

Standards of Conduct **for Employees** *of the Executive* **Branch**

5 CFR § 2635.201 –

(a) Overview. This subpart contains standards that prohibit an employee from soliciting or accepting any gift from a prohibited source or any gift given because of the employee's official position, unless the item is excluded from the definition of a gift or falls within one of the exceptions set forth in this subpart.

(b) Considerations for declining otherwise permissible gifts.

(1) Every employee has a fundamental responsibility to the United States and its citizens to place loyalty to the Constitution, laws, and ethical principles above private gain. An employee's actions should promote the public's trust that this responsibility is being met. For this reason, employees should consider declining otherwise permissible gifts if they believe that a reasonable person with knowledge of the relevant facts would question the employee's integrity or impartiality as a result of accepting the gift.

(2) An employee who is considering whether acceptance of a gift would lead a reasonable person with knowledge of the relevant facts to question his or her integrity or impartiality may consider, among other relevant factors, whether: (i) The gift has a high market value; (ii) The timing of the gift creates the appearance that the donor is seeking to influence an official action; (iii) The gift was provided by a person who has interests that may be substantially affected by the performance or nonperformance of the

employee's official duties; and (iv) Acceptance of the gift would provide the donor with significantly disproportionate access.

* * *

(4) Employees who have questions regarding this subpart ... should seek advice from an agency ethics official. **5 CFR § 2635.202 –**

(a) Except as provided in this [regulation], an employee shall not, directly or indirectly, solicit or accept a gift:

> (1)   From a prohibited source;

> (2)   Given because of the employee's official position.

5 CFR § 2635.204(b) –

An employee may accept a gift given under circumstances which make it clear that the gift is motivated by a family relationship or personal friendship rather than the position of the employee. Relevant factors in making such a determination include the history of the relationship and whether the family member or friend personally pays for the gift.

Example 3 to paragraph (b): A Peace Corps employee enjoys using a social media site on the internet in his personal capacity outside of work. He has used the site to keep in touch with friends, neighbors, coworkers, professional contacts, and other individuals he has met over the years through both work and personal activities. One of these individuals works for a contractor that provides language services to the Peace Corps. The employee was acting in his official capacity when he met the individual at a meeting to discuss a matter related to the contract between their respective employers. Thereafter, the two communicated occasionally regarding contract matters. They later also granted one another access to join their social media networks through their respective social media accounts. However, they did not communicate further in their personal capacities, carry on extensive personal interactions, or meet socially outside of work. One day, the individual, whose employer continues to serve as a Peace Corps contractor, contacts the employee to offer him a pair of concert tickets worth $30 apiece. Although the employee and the individual are connected through social media, the circumstances do not demonstrate that the gift was clearly motivated by a personal relationship, rather than the position of the employee, and therefore the employee may not accept the gift pursuant to paragraph (b) of this section.

5 CFR § 2635.702 –

An employee shall not use his public office for his own private gain, for the endorsement of any product, service or enterprise, or for the private gain of friends, relatives, or persons with whom the employee is affiliated in a nongovernmental capacity, including nonprofit organizations of which the employee is an officer or member, and persons with whom the employee has or seeks employment or business relations.

5 CFR § 2635.704 –

An employee has a duty to protect and conserve Government property and shall not use such property, or allow its use, for other than authorized purposes.

5 CFR § 2635.705 –

(a)   Unless authorized in accordance with law or regulations to use such time for other purposes, an employee shall use official time in an honest effort to perform official duties. An employee not under a leave system, including a Presidential appointee exempted under 5 U.S.C. 6301(2), has an obligation to expend an honest effort and a reasonable portion of his time in the performance of official duties;

(b)   An employee shall not encourage, direct, coerce, or request a subordinate to use official time to perform activities other than those required in the performance of official duties or authorized in accordance with law or regulation.

Office of Government Ethics (OGE) – OGE Letter, March 21, 2006. A letter sent by OGE in response to a request for an advisory opinion stated, in part, under the section titled "Legal Authority":

The Standards of Conduct ban an employee's receipt of gifts given by prohibited sources or because of one's official position.... Gifts clearly motivated by a family relationship or private friendship, however, are excluded from this prohibition.... An employee may not use this exception to solicit or coerce the offering of a gift.... Where a personal relationship develops from an on-going work relationship, it can be very difficult to clearly establish that the gift is not being given because of the employee's official position.... Therefore, an employee bears a considerable burden in establishing that a gift is based on a personal relationship rather than the employee's Government position.... Factors indicating a personal relationship include the length of time of the relationship, the intimacy of the relationship including any family interaction, the nature of personal activities outside the work context, and the frequency of outside contacts.

VA Designated Agency Ethics Official – Memorandum to All VA Employees

issued by Tammy Kennedy on February 23, 2017, stated,

1.   Effective January 1, 2017, the U.S. Office of Government Ethics (OGE) amended the Standards of Ethical Conduct for Employees of the Executive

Branch (the Standards) regulations with regards to gifts. The most significant revision affects the process for how we as Federal employees are to review gifts from sources outside of the Federal Government to determine if we may accept the gift. OGE has added a values-based element to the process, concerned that employees may not sufficiently analyze appearance issues and instead may focus exclusively on whether a gift can be accepted under a regulatory gift exception.

2.   The standards now require that when offered a gift from someone outside the Government the employee must make a ***preliminary*** determination of whether the employee should accept the gift. Specifically, the employee is asked to consider whether a reasonable person with knowledge of the relevant facts would question the employee's impartiality or integrity, or the impartiality or integrity of VA's programs and operations, as a result of accepting the gift.

3.   In making this preliminary determination, the employee must consider four factors: value, timing, identification of donor, and access to employees of the Department. Does the offered gift have a high market value? Does the timing of the gift create the appearance that the donor is seeking to influence an official action? Does the donor have interests that may be substantially affected by the performance or nonperformance of the employee's official duties? Would acceptance of the gift provide the donor with significantly disproportionate access to VA or VA employees?

4.   After taking these factors into consideration if the employee believes that a reasonable person would question the employee's integrity or impartiality or the integrity or impartiality of VA programs or operations, then the employee should not accept the gift. Only if the employee believes that the employee's or VA's integrity will not be questioned should the employee then move on to the question of whether acceptance of the gift is legal.

VA's Ethics Specialty Team can assist with this preliminary determination as well as the subsequent question of the legality of acceptance.

5.   Should you have any questions, the contact information for [the Ethics Specialty Team] is attached.

Federal Travel Regulations and VA Travel Policy

41 CFR § 300-3.1 – Defines invitational travel as

Authorized travel of individuals either not employed or employed (under 5 U.S.C. § 5703) intermittently in the Government service… when they are acting in a capacity that is directly related to, or in connection with, official activities of the Government. Travel allowances authorized for such persons are the same as those normally authorized for employees in connection with TDY.

VA Travel Administration, Volume XIV, Chapter 1, Section 010202, February 2017 –

Subsection (B)(1) Invitational travel involves VA paying for the travel of a non-Federal employee, a Federal employee traveling in a non-duty status, or consultants (not under an agreement or contract with VA).… Invitational travelers are not considered to have an "official permanent duty station" within the general meaning of that term. However, these individuals may be allowed travel and transportation expenses while traveling on official business for the Government away from their home or regular place of business and while at the place of employment or service for the Government.

41 CFR §§ 301-2.2, 301-2.3, 301-2.4 –

(301-2.2) [an] agency may pay only those expenses essential to the transaction of official business.…

(301-2.3) [an employee] must exercise the same care in incurring expenses that a prudent person would exercise if traveling on personal business.

(301-2.4) [the] agency will not pay for excess costs resulting from circuitous routes, delays, luxury accommodations or services unnecessary or unjustified in the performance of official business.

41 CFR § 301-11.21 –

> (a)   In general, [an employee] will be reimbursed as long as [the employee's] travel status requires [their] stay to include a non-workday, (e.g., if [the employee is] on travel through Friday and again starting Monday [they] will be reimbursed for Saturday and Sunday), however, [the] agency should determine the most cost effective situation (i.e., remaining in a travel status and paying per diem or actual expenses or permitting [the employee to] return to [their] official station).

> (b)   [The employee's] agency will determine whether [the employee] will be reimbursed for non-workdays when [they] take leave immediately (e.g., Friday or Monday) before or after the non-workday(s).

VA Travel Administration, Volume XIV, Chapter 1, Appendix E, May 2013, sets forth specific procedures to be followed when combining personal and official travel. Section B (2) of Appendix E instructs employees to "use a Travel Cost Comparison Worksheet to compare official travel to official/personal travel." The worksheet is then "reviewed as the cost comparison by [the] approving official."

***Federal* Regulations *and VA Policy for* Electronic Mail Records**

Administrative Investigation – VA Secretary and Delegation Travel to Europe

36 CFR § 1234.34 –

Electronic records may be destroyed only in accordance with a records disposition schedule approved by the Archivist of the United States, including General Records Schedules.

VA Directive 6301, Procedures for Handling Electronic Mail Records –

(2)(a) All Government employees and contractors are required by law to make and preserve records containing adequate and proper documentation of the organization, functions, policies, decisions, procedures, and essential transactions of the agency. In addition, Federal regulations govern the life cycle of these records: they must be properly stored, preserved, and available for retrieval, and may be disposed of only in accordance with authorized records control schedules.

*   *   *

(3)(b) Users of VA electronic mail systems will not alter or improperly dispose of any electronic mail message, record of transmission and receipt date, or attachment (such as a document) which meets the definition of a Federal record received or created on these systems. **VA Handbook 6301, Electronic Mail Records** –

(2)(f) All VA employees are subject to the provisions of 36 CFR … as it pertains to electronic mail.

(2)(g) Electronic mail messages are records when they are made by VA under Federal law or in connection with public business; and are preserved or are appropriate for preservation as evidence of organization, functions, policies, decisions, procedures, operations, or other activities of the Government, or because of the information value of the data in them.

(2)(h) Prior to deletion of an electronic mail message, independent consideration will be made by the sender and the person who receives the electronic mail message whether or not it meets the definition of a Federal record. If so, then the message, along with essential transmission and receipt data must be preserved for each electronic mail record in order for the context of the message to be understood.

Administrative Investigation — VA Secretary and Delegation Travel to Europe

Appendix   B

Excerpted Itinerary from Official Trip Book[53]

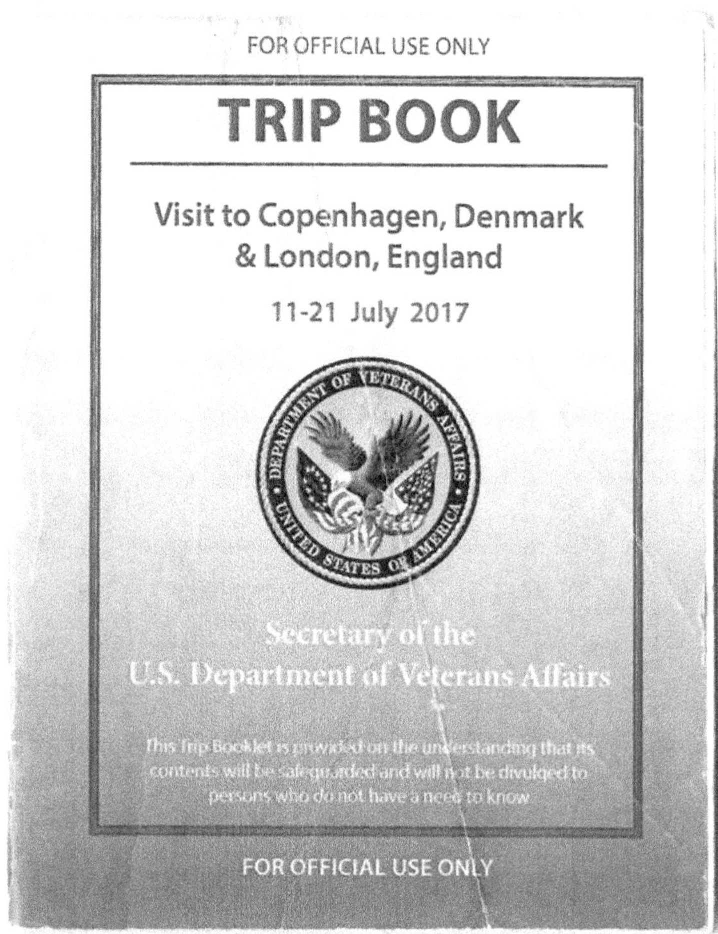

---

[53] OIG did not verify each scheduled activity in order to determine whether there were any deviations from the planned itinerary.

London Ministerial Summit Briefing

- Day One – PTSD / Veteran Suicide
- Day Two – Access to Care

Copenhagen/London Gift Exchanges

- SECVA Presenting Denmark's Minister of Defense [redacted] with Medallion Box
- United Kingdom
  - United Kingdom: Rt Hon [redacted] MP: Minister for Defence People and Veterans – Medallion Box
  - Canada: The Hon [redacted] Minister of Veterans Affairs and Associate Minister of National Defence - Coin Box
  - New Zealand: [redacted] Head of Veterans' Affairs, New Zealand - Coin Box
  - Australia: The Hon [redacted] MP. Minister for Veterans' Affairs, Defence Personnel, Cyber Security and ANZAC Centenary - Coin Box

---

Emergency Contact Information Denmark

Duty Officer: +45 [redacted]
Taxi Nord: +45 4848 4848
Danish Emergency Services
Fire/Police/Ambulance 112

12

FOR OFFICIAL USE ONLY

Tuesday, July 11, 2017 Weather: New York, NY; Copenhagen, Denmark		Attire: Casual — H 87°, L 65° - T-Storms & Cloud; H 62°, L 51° - Showers AM & Mostly Cloudy
TIME	**ACTIVITY**	**LOCATION**
14:00 - 14:30	**ERT/ARRIVE AT NEW YORK KENNEDY AIRPORT (JFK)** Drive time: 14.7mil / 30min	New York Kennedy Airport (JFK)
16:35 (EDT)	**WHEELS-UP TO COPENHAGEN, DENMARK KASTRUP (CPH) AIRPORT** Delta 0218, Flight time: 8hr 25min	
Wednesday, July 12, 2017 Weather: Copenhagen, Denmark		**Attire: Casual — H 63°, L 52° - Mostly Sunny**
Arrive 07:00	**Arrive in Copenhagen.** *Will be met on arrival by Acting Charge d' Affaires [redacted] Defense Attache CAPT [redacted] and Control Officer POL [redacted] Denmark security and escorted to Royal Arrivals Lounge. Baggage will be brought to Royal Lounge for delegation to claim (TBD).*	Copenhagen Airport, Kastrup
TBD	**Motorcade Transport to Crowne Plaza Hotel.** *You will claim your baggage at the Royal Lounge and it will follow to the hotel.*	Crowne Plaza Copenhagen Towers Copenhagen – 2300 S, Denmark +45-88-776655
TBD	**Check-in to Crowne Plaza Copenhagen Towers**	Crowne Plaza Copenhagen Towers
TBD	**EXECUTIVE TIME**	Crowne Plaza Copenhagen Towers
11:10–11:30	**Transport to Frederik's Church**	Frederiksgade 4, Copenhagen 1265, Denmark
11:30–11:40	**Frederik's Church**	Frederiksgade 4, Copenhagen 1265, Denmark
11:40–11:50	**Walk to Amalienborg Palace**	Amalienborg Palace Square, Copenhagen 1257, Denmark

FOR OFFICIAL USE ONLY

13

Administrative Investigation—VA Secretary and Delegation Travel to Europe

TIME	ACTIVITY	LOCATION
11:50–12:15	**Amalienborg Palace for Changing of the Guard** (12pm)	Amalienborg Palace Square, Copenhagen 1257, Denmark
12:15–12:25	**Transport to Lunch at Kanal Cafeen**	Kanal Cafeen Frederiksholms Kanal 18, Copenhagen 1220, Denmark
12:25–13:25	**Lunch at Kanal Cafeen** *Right Across from Christiansborg Palace	Kanal Cafeen Frederiksholms Kanal 18, Copenhagen 1220, Denmark
13:25-13:30	**Transport to Christiansborg Palace** *(short walk)*	Prins Joergens Gaard 1, Copenhagen 1218, Denmark
13:30-14:30	**Christiansborg Palace Self-Guided Tour**	Prins Joergens Gaard 1, Copenhagen 1218, Denmark
14:30-14:40	**Transport to Rosenborg Castle**	Rosenborg Castle Oster Voldgade 4A, Copenhagen 1350, Denmark
14:40-15:40	**Rosenborg Castle**	Rosenborg Castle Oster Voldgade 4A, Copenhagen 1350, Denmark
15:40-15:50	**Transport to Nyhavn**	Nyhavn 1F, 1051 København K, Denmark
16:00- 17:00	**Copenhagen Canal Boat Tour from Nyhavn** Gabe to coordinate canal boat tour tickets. *Will See Little Mermaid Statue (in the harbor) from the boat	Nyhavn 1F, 1051 København K, Denmark
17:00-17:40	**Walk around Nyhavn**	Nyhavn 1F, 1051 København K, Denmark
17:40-17:50	**Short walk to Ved Stranden 10-Vinhandel and Bar**	Ved Stranden 10 Vinhandel og Bar, Ved Stranden 10, 1061 København K, Denmark

TIME	ACTIVITY	LOCATION
18:00-19:30	**Ved Stranden 10-Vinhandel and Bar**	Ved Stranden 10 Vinhandel og Bar, Ved Stranden 10, 1061 København K, Denmark
19:30-19:50	**Depart for Hotel** RON	Crowne Plaza Copenhagen Towers Copenhagen – 2300 S, Denmark +45-88-776655

Thursday, July 13,2017 **Weather:** Copenhagen, Denmark	**Attire:** Business H-69°; L-58°-Mostly Cloudy

Please bring passport as photo identification for Danish ministries July 13-14

TIME	ACTIVITY	LOCATION
08:30-09:00	**Depart Hotel to Danish MOD**	Ministry of Defence (Forsvarsministeriet), Holmens Kanal 42, Copenhagen K
09:00	**Meeting with Danish Ministry of Defense –** **Welcome** ▮▮▮▮ Permanent Secretary of State for Defence	Ministry of Defence (Forsvarsministeriet), Holmens Kanal 42, Copenhagen K
09:05-09:25	**Briefing on the Danish Veterans Policy and Health Care System** ▮▮▮▮ Deputy Permanent Secretary of State for Defence and head of Personnel and Administration Division.	Ministry of Defence
09:25-09:45	**Briefing on the role of The Danish Veterans Centre** - Colonel ▮▮▮▮ CO Danish Veterans Centre	Ministry of Defence
09:45-10:30	**Q's and A's**	Ministry of Defence

Administrative Investigation — VA Secretary and Delegation Travel to Europe

TIME	ACTIVITY	LOCATION
10:30-10:45	**Transport to Veterans Home Copenhagen**	Veterans Home Copenhagen (Veteranhjem København), Roskildevej 54, 2000 Frederiksberg
10:45-11:15	**Visit at Veterans Home Copenhagen** -Introduction by Chairman of the Foundation of Danish Veterans Homes, Mr.	Veterans Home Copenhagen
11:15-11:30	**Transport to The Citadel** (Kastellet)	The Citadel (Kastellet), Gl. Hovedvagt, Kastellet 1, 2100 Copenhagen
11:30-11:50	**Wreath Laying Ceremony** -US Secretary of Veterans Affairs Dr. Shulkin laying the wreath with Defense Attache CAPT	The Monument for the Danish International Engagement after 1948, The Citadel
11:50-12:30	**Transport to Humlebæk Harbor** -Short walk to Bolettes Gæstebud	Humlebæk Harbor Havnevej, 3050 Humlebæk
12:30-14:15	**Lunch hosted by Danish Minister of Defence** -Mr.	"Bolettes Gæstebud", Humlebæk
14:15-14:30	**Transport to Louisiana Museum of Modern Art, Humlebæk**	Louisiana Museum of Modern Art, Gl. Strandvej, 3050 Humlebæk
14:30-15:30	**Guided visit to Louisiana Museum of Modern Art, Humlebæk** - By proposal of Danish MOD	Louisiana Museum of Modern Art, Gl. Strandvej, 3050 Humlebæk
15:30-16:00	**Transport to Frederiksborg Castle**	Frederiksborg Slot 10, Hillerod 3400, Denmark
16:00-17:15	**Frederiksborg Castle**	Frederiksborg Slot 10, Hillerod 3400, Denmark
17:15-18:00	**Transport back to hotel**	Crowne Plaza Copenhagen Towers Copenhagen — 2300 S, Denmark +45-88-776655
18:00-18:40	**Buffer Time / Executive Time / Prepare for Dinner**	Crowne Plaza Copenhagen Towers

TIME	ACTIVITY	LOCATION
18:40-19:00	**Transport to dinner**	Location TBD
19:00 – 20:30	**Dinner at Nimb Brasserie**	Nimb Brasserie — Tivoli Gardens
20:30-21:30	**Walk to Tivoli after dinner.** Tickets required for entry cost DKK 108; Gabe Gough to coordinate.	Tivoli Gardens, Vesterbrogade 3, 1630 København V, Denmark
21:30-21:50	**Depart for Hotel.** RON Pick up point TBC with advance — Tivoli exit on H.C. Andersen side of park (near Radhusplads)	Crowne Plaza Copenhagen Towers Copenhagen — 2300 S, Denmark +45-88-776655

Please bring passport as photo identification for Danish ministries July 13-14

Friday, July 14, 2017
Weather: Copenhagen, Denmark
Attires: Business
H 68° L 54° Mostly Cloudy

TIME	ACTIVITY	LOCATION
8:30	**Depart for Ministry of Foreign Affairs for Meeting with Ministry of Health**	Ministry of Foreign Affairs Asiatisk Plads #2
09:00-11:30	**Meeting with Ministry of Health** + Explanation of the Danish healthcare system + Access to Care (understand how Denmark has managed the prioritization of care, wait times, center of excellence, etc) + National Digitalization strategy (interested in Denmark's progress as well as implementation of EHR and telemedicine)	Ministry of Foreign Affairs

TIME	ACTIVITY	LOCATION
09:00-11:30 (Cont'd)	• Modernization/state-of-the-art hospitals (learn about modernization of existing facilities as well as design/construction of new hospitals) • National Strategy for Personalized Medicine and the Use of Health Data • Discussion / Q&As	Ministry of Foreign Affairs
11:30-11:45	**Walk to lunch** (weather permitting)	Borsen (Stock Exchange) building
11:45-13:30	**Roundtable Lunch with CEO's of Danish Healthcare Companies.** *Suggested discussion topic: Veterans Affairs' strategy for health and how VA will address and seek solutions for the growing aging population and management of increased chronic disease(s)* **Participants:** Host: ▓▓▓▓▓▓▓ Ambassador & State Secretary for Trade, Ministry of Foreign Affairs ▓▓▓▓▓▓▓ Counselor & Senior Advisor - Danish Embassy, Washington, D.C. ▓▓▓▓▓▓▓ Deputy Political Chief - US Embassy Copenhagen ▓▓▓▓▓▓▓ Political Officer - US Embassy ▓▓▓▓▓▓▓ Executive Vice President & CCO - Ambu ▓▓▓▓▓▓▓ President & CEO - Coloplast	Location in Copenhagen TBD

TIME	ACTIVITY	LOCATION
11:45-13:30 (Cont'd)	▓▓▓▓▓▓▓ President & CEO - GN Hearing ▓▓▓▓▓▓▓ President & CEO - LEO Pharma ▓▓▓▓▓▓▓ President & CEO - Oticon ▓▓▓▓▓▓▓ Director, Healthcare - Systematic ▓▓▓▓▓▓▓ Senior Vice President, Sales and Marketing – Widex ▓▓▓▓▓▓▓ Deputy Executive Director - Dansk Erhverv ▓▓▓▓▓▓▓ CEO - Healthcare Denmark	Location in Copenhagen TBD
13:30-13:45	**Transport to Rigshospitalet**	Rigshospitalet Blegdamsvej 9, Copenhagen
13:45-16:30	Tour of Rigshospitalet Introduction to research/teaching hospital • Example of Danish healthcare delivery in practice • Visits to 2-3 leading departments • Discussion of programs (clinical, research, etc) for possible collaboration	Rigshospitalet Blegdamsvej 9, Copenhagen
16:30-16:45	**Transport to Strøget** (shopping area)	Crowne Plaza Copenhagen Towers Copenhagen – 2300 S, Denmark +45-88-776655

TIME	ACTIVITY	LOCATION
16:45-18:00	Strøget	Strøget, 1160 København, Denmark
18:00-18:15	Walk to dinner location Cafe Norden	Oestergade 61, Copenhagen 1100, Denmark
18:15-19:30	Cafe Norden	Oestergade 61, Copenhagen 1100, Denmark
19:30-19:45	Transport to Hotel	Crowne Plaza Copenhagen Towers Copenhagen – 2300 S, Denmark +45-88-776655

Saturday, July 15, 2017
Weather: Copenhagen, Denmark / London, England
Attire: Casual
H-67°; L-56° - Mostly Sunny
H-70°; L-54° - Partly Cloudy

TIME	ACTIVITY	LOCATION
0500-0530	Baggage call in Copenhagen: *(check out and depart for airport by NLT 0530)*	Hotel lobby
05:30	Depart for Airport to arrive at CPH Royal Lounge *(NLT 0550)*	Copenhagen Airport, Kastrup
07:20	Wheels up to London *British Airways 0811*	Copenhagen Airport, Kastrup
08:35	Arrive Heathrow International Airport	Heathrow International Airport
09:35-10:35	Transport to Royal Horseguards Hotel	Royal Horseguards Hotel 2 Whitehall Court, Whitehall London: +44 800 330 8090
10:35	Check-in to Royal Horseguards Hotel	Royal Horseguards Hotel
10:35-11:40	EXECUTIVE TIME	Royal Horseguards Hotel

TIME	ACTIVITY	LOCATION
11:40-12:30	Transport to Wimbledon	Church Road, Wimbledon | All England Lawn Tennis & Croquet Club, London SW19 5A
12:30-17:30	Wimbledon *Juniors from 11am on outside courts, all other main draw matches from 11.30am, 1pm on Centre and No.1 Courts.* • 2pm - Ladies' Singles final • Gentlemen's Doubles final • Ladies' Doubles final • Girls' Singles final • Wheelchair Ladies' Singles final • Wheelchair Gentlemen's Doubles final • Mixed Doubles semi-finals • Boys' and Girls' Doubles semi-finals • Invitation Doubles	Church Road, Wimbledon | All England Lawn Tennis & Croquet Club, London SW19 5A
17:30-18:15	Transport to Dinner at Al Duca	Al Duca 4-5 Duke of York Street | St James, London SW1Y 6LA, England
18:30-19:30	Dinner at Al Duca	Al Duca 4-5 Duke of York Street | St James, London SW1Y 6LA, England
TBD	Transport to Trafalgar Square	Trafalgar Square, London WC2N 5DN, UK
TBD	Transport to Hotel	Royal Horseguards Hotel 2 Whitehall Court, Whitehall London: +44 800 330 8090

Administrative Investigation – VA Secretary and Delegation Travel to Europe

Sunrday, July 16, 2017
Weather: London, England
Attire: Casual
H-70°; L-53° -Partly Cloudy

TIME	ACTIVITY	LOCATION
09:20-09:30	Short walk to Churchill War Room	Clive Steps | King Charles Street, London SW1A 2AQ, England
09:30-11:00	Churchill War Room	Clive Steps | King Charles Street, London SW1A 2AQ, England
11:00-11:20	Walk through St. James Park to Buckingham Palace	
11:20-11:35	Buckingham Palace + Photo Stop	Buckingham Palace Road, London SW1A 1AA, England
11:35-11:45	Walk through Buckingham Palace Gardens to Wellington Arch on way to Hyde Park	
11:45-12:25	Walk through Hyde Park to Kensington Palace	
12:25-13:15	The Honest Sausage	Broad Walk | Kensington Gardens, London W8 0AB, England
13:15-14:45	Kensington Palace	Kensington Gardens, London W8 4PX, England
14:45-15:30	Transport to Westminster Abbey	Broad Sanctuary, London SW1P 3PA, England
14:45-15:30	Westminster Abbey	Broad Sanctuary, London SW1P 3PA, England
15:30-15:45	Walk to Westminster Pier	Westminster Pier, Victoria Embankment, London SW1A 2JH
16:00-17:00	Thames River Cruise to Greenwich Pier	Greenwich Pier, Lower
17:10-17:40	Dinner in Greenwich	TBD
17:40-18:50	Dinner	TBD

TIME	ACTIVITY	LOCATION
TBD	Transport to Piccadilly Circus	London W1J 9HS, England
TBD	Evening in Piccadilly Circus	London W1J 9HS, England
TBD	Transport to Hotel	Royal Horseguards Hotel 2 Whitehall Court, Whitehall London: +44 800 330 8090

Monday, July 17, 2017
Weather: London, England
Attire: Casual
H-71°; L-55° -Showers, Mostly Cloudy

TIME	ACTIVITY	LOCATION
08:15-08:30	Transport to St. Paul's Cathedral	St. Paul's Cathedral, St. Paul's Churchyard, London EC4M 8AD, UK
08:30-09:30	St. Paul's Cathedral	St. Paul's Cathedral, St. Paul's Churchyard, London EC4M 8AD, UK
09:30-09:45	Transport to Tower of London	Tower Hill, London EC3N 4AB, England
09:45-11:30	Tower of London	Tower Hill, London EC3N 4AB, England
11:30-11:40	Walk to Tower Bridge	Tower Bridge, London SE1 2AA, UK
11:40-12:40	Tower Bridge	Tower Bridge, London SE1 2AA, UK
12:40-12:50	Transport to Pizza Express	24 New Globe Walk | Unit 1 Benbow House, London SE1 9DS, England
12:50-13:30	Pizza Express	24 New Globe Walk | Unit 1 Benbow House, London SE1 9DS, England

TIME	ACTIVITY	LOCATION
13:30-13:35	Walk to Shakespeare's Globe	21 New Globe Walk, London SE1 9DT, England
13:35-14:35	Shakespeare's Globe	21 New Globe Walk, London SE1 9DT, England
14:35-14:55	Transport to Hotel	Royal Horseguards Hotel 2 Whitehall Court, Whitehall London: +44 800 330 8090
14:55-17:40	EXECUTIVE TIME	Royal Horseguards Hotel
18:00-18:15	Transport to Dinner	The Archduke, 153 Concert Hall Approach, Lambeth, London SE1 8XU, UK
18:15-19:30	Dinner at the Archduke	The Archduke, 153 Concert Hall Approach, Lambeth, London SE1 8XU, UK
19:30-19:40	Transport to London Eye	London Eye, Lambeth, London SE1 7GL, United Kingdom
19:45-20:15	London Eye (£18.70)	London Eye, Lambeth, London SE1 7GL, United Kingdom
20:30-21:00	Transport to Ceremony of the Keys	Ceremony of the Keys, Tower Of London, St Katharine's & Wapping, London EC3N 4AB, UK

TIME	ACTIVITY	LOCATION
21:15-22:15	**Ceremony of the Keys** Met and escorted by Duty Governor, [redacted] is an Afghanistan Veteran and former member of the Scots Guards. "I was [redacted]	Ceremony of the Keys, Tower Of London, St Katharine's & Wapping, London EC3N 4AB, UK
22:25-23:40	Transport to Hotel	Royal Horseguards Hotel 2 Whitehall Court, Whitehall London: +44 800 330 8090

Administrative Investigation — VA Secretary and Delegation Travel to Europe

| Tuesday, July 18, 2017 | | Attire: AM - Casual / PM - Business |
| Weather: London, England | | H-71°, L-55° - Showers, Mostly Cloudy |

TIME	ACTIVITY	LOCATION
08:20-09:20	Transport to Windsor Castle	23 Francis Street, Windsor SL4 1NJ, England
09:30-11:30	Windsor Castle • 11am: Changing of the Guard	23 Francis Street, Windsor SL4 1NJ, England
11:30-11:40	Walk to Lunch at Cote Brasserie	Cote Brasserie - Windsor 71-72 High Street	Eton, Windsor SL4 6AA, England
11:40-12:40	Lunch at Cote Brasserie - Windsor	Cote Brasserie - Windsor 71-72 High Street	Eton, Windsor SL4 6AA, England
12:40-13:40	Transport to Royal Horseguards Hotel	Royal Horseguards Hotel 2 Whitehall Court, Whitehall London: +44 800 330 8090
13:40-17:40	EXECUTIVE TIME	Royal Horseguards Hotel 2 Whitehall Court, Whitehall London: +44 800 330 8090
17:45-18:00	Walk to 10 Downing Street • Prime Minister will not be in attendance	
		10 Downing Street
18:00-19:30	Evening Reception for Summit delegates and guests at Prime Minister's Residence	10 Downing Street
	Transport to Dinner	TBD
	Dinner	TBD
	Transport to Royal Horseguards Hotel	Royal Horseguards Hotel 2 Whitehall Court, Whitehall London: +44 800 330 8090

| Wednesday, July 19, 2017 | | Attire: Business | |
| Weather: London, England | | H-71°; L-54° -Partly Cloudy | |

TIME	AGENDA ITEM	LOCATION	PRESENTER
0800 (30 mins)	Bus from hotel to Royal Hospital Chelsea (RHC)		
0830 (25 mins)	Tea and Coffee	RHC	
0855 (5 mins)	Welcome and Opening Address	RHC	(UK)
0900 (40 mins)	UK Mental Health Strategy 20 min Presentation followed by 20 min Discussion	RHC	(UK)
0940 (60 mins)	Veterans Mental Health: Facts, Myths and Challenges 30 min Presentation followed by 30 min Discussion	RHC	(UK)
1040 (20 mins)	Morning Tea/Coffee	RHC	
1100 (60 mins)	Post-Traumatic Stress Disorder – Veterans' Suicide 20 min Presentation followed by 40 min Discussion	RHC	Secretary Shulkin (USA)
1200 (60 mins)	Barriers to Effective Mental Health Treatment in the Veteran Population 20 min Presentation followed by 40 min Discussion	RHC	(AUS)
1300 (60 mins)	Lunch – Great Hall (Ministers with Chelsea Pensioners) and State Apartments	RHC	

VA Office of Inspector General

Administrative Investigation — VA Secretary and Delegation Travel to Europe

TIME	AGENDA ITEM	LOCATION	PRESENTER
1400 (60 mins)	Alternative therapies - Cannabis, Service Dogs and Equine Therapy 20 min Presentation followed by 40 min Discussion	RHC	TBD (CAN)
1500 (60 mins)	Veteran- centric rehabilitation; by them, with them, for them. Reaching out with a cross sector approach offering ways to recover, rebuild, and enable a good life. 20 min Presentation followed by 40 min Discussion	RHC	(NZ)
1600 (80 mins)	Mental Health Care: The UK Approach – NHS Commissioning, delivery and collaboration with the third sector. 20 Min + 20 min presentation followed by 40 min Discussion	RHC	(UK)
1735 (30 mins)	Bus to hotel		
1805 – 1915 (70 mins)	Free time	Hotel	
1915 - 1930 (30 mins)	Bus from hotel to Lancaster House		
1930 (90 mins)	Dinner at Lancaster House	LH	
2100 (15 mins)	Bus to hotel		

Thursday, July 20, 2017   **Attire:** Business
Weather: London, England   H-71°; L-54° -Mostly Sunny

TIME	AGENDA ITEM	LOCATION	PRESNETER
0800 (30 mins)	Bus from hotel to Stoll		
0830 (60mins)	Introduction to Stoll and Poppy Factory services and site tour	Stoll	Stoll/Poppy Factory (UK)
0930 (15 mins)	Bus to RHC		
1000 (60 mins)	Old problems and new opportunities. Contemporary veterans are a new demographic with different expectations. Contemporary conflict brings new exposures and new technology is bringing new opportunities. 20 min Presentation followed by 40 min Discussion	RHC	(NZ)
1100 (60 mins)	The continuum of support for transition from military service 20 min Presentation followed by 40 min Discussion	RHC	TBD (CAN)
1200 (60 mins)	Lunch – State Apartments	RHC	
1300 (60 mins)	Tour of Royal Hospital Chelsea by the Governor	RHC	(UK)
1400 (60 mins)	Rehabilitation Initiatives and Proactive Interventions 20 min Presentation followed by 40 min Discussion	RHC	(AUS)
1500 (60 mins)	Access to care for Veterans 20 min Presentation followed by 40 min Discussion	RHC	Secretary Shulkin (USA)

VA Office of Inspector General

Administrative Investigation — VA Secretary and Delegation Travel to Europe

TIME	AGENDA ITEM	LOCATION	PRESNETER
1600 (20 mins)	**Afternoon tea/coffee – State Apartments**	RHC	
1620 (35 mins)	**The importance of the Third Sector** 20 min Presentation followed by 15 min Discussion	RHC	(UK)
1655 (35 mins)	**UK Armed Forces Covenant** 20 min Presentation followed by 15 min Discussion	RHC	(UK)
1730 (25mins)	**Conference Closing Remarks and Next Steps** 5 min each delegation	RHC	Delegation leads
1800 (25mins)	**Bus to hotel**		
1825	**Dinner**		TBD

Friday, July 21, 2017 — Attire: Casual
Weather: London, England
Washington, DC

TIME	ACTIVITY	LOCATION
Morning	**OPEN**	TBD
14:15-15:15	**Depart for Heathrow Airport**	Hounslow TW6, England
16:40	**Wheels up to IAD** • United Airlines, Flight #0925 • Non-Stop: 8 hours 5 minutes	
19:45	**Arrive IAD**	
TBD	Transport to Residence	

July 24th: Security Debrief

DEPARTMENT OF STATE

U.S. Embassy Copenhagen
Dag Hammarskjölds Allé 24 2100 Copenhagen Denmark
Telephone: +(45) 3341 7100
Emergency After Hours Telephone +(45) 3341 7100
Fax +(45) 3538 9616
Email: @State.gov
U.S. Embassy Copenhagen
Smart Travel Enrollment Program
https://step.state.gov/step/

TRAVEL

❖ VA employees with a security clearance (Secret/Top Secret) are required to make notification of **ALL** foreign travel, conducted for either **OFFICIAL** or **PERSONAL** purpose, two weeks in advance to the Insider Threat Program. These employees will be required to receive a travel briefong prior to foreign travel and will be subject to a security debrief upon completion of foreign travel.

❖ VA employees are prohibited from taking government furnished electronic devices (laptops, tablets, phones) on foreogn travel unless cleared by their supervisor and Office Information Technology (OIT) support. If an employee does bring electronic devices, including personally owened, it is recommended to avoid using public Wi-Fi networks whenever possible.

Appendix C

Comments

The Office of Inspector General received two written responses from the VA Secretary and one from the VA Deputy Secretary, which are appended in full to this report as Appendices D, E, and F, respectively.

The following comments were submitted by VA, through the Deputy Secretary, in response to the recommendations in the Office of Inspector General's Report:

Recommendation 1: Secretary Shulkin reimburses the $4,312 paid by VA to cover Dr. Bari's travel costs.

Comments: The Secretary does not agree with the OIG conclusions of fact and law relating to this recommendation as presented in the OIG report, however he will consult with the Office of General Counsel and if it is determined that he should reimburse the Department for any part of Dr. Bari's travel costs he will do so.

Recommendation 2: Secretary Shulkin consults with the Office of General Counsel to determine the value of the Wimbledon tickets; grounds pass; and any food, parking, and other tangible benefits Ms. Gosling provided in connection with Wimbledon and reimburse that amount to her. If Ms. Gosling declines to accept reimbursement, Secretary Shulkin reimburses such amount to the US Treasury.

Comments: The Secretary does not agree with the OIG conclusions of fact and law relating to this recommendation, however, he will consult with the Office of General Counsel and if it is determined that he should reimburse Ms. Gosling for any aspect of his attendance at Wimbledon, he will do so. (If Ms. Gosling declines to accept reimbursement, the Secretary will reimburse such amount to the U.S. Treasury.)

Recommendation 3: The Deputy Secretary of Veterans Affairs confers with the Offices of General Counsel, Human Resources, and Accountability and Whistleblower Protection to determine the appropriate administrative action to take, if any, against Ms. Wright Simpson and any other individuals associated with the Europe trip.

Appendix C

> **Comments:** The Department has been inappropriately compelled and had an inadequate opportunity to review and respond to the Inspector General's report and the evidence that accompanied it. When the Department has completed its review the Deputy Secretary will in inform OIG as to whether it will accept this recommendation.
>
> **Recommendation 4:** The Deputy Secretary of Veterans Affairs ensures that a thorough audit is conducted of the expense vouchers, travel authorizations, and the time and attendance records for all travelers on the Europe trip. Any overpayments should be reimbursed to VA by the traveler and any required leave adjustments should be made. Detailed results of the audits, including supporting documentation, shall be provided to the Office of Inspector General no later than thirty days following the publication of this report.
>
> **Comments:** The Department has been inappropriately compelled and had an inadequate opportunity to review and respond to the Inspector General's report and the evidence that accompanied it. When the Department has completed its review the Deputy Secretary will in inform OIG as to whether it will accept this recommendation.
>
> **Recommendation 5:** The Deputy Secretary of Veterans Affairs ensures that the Office of General Counsel (i) reviews and enhances the training provided to staff on travel planning, approvals, and the solicitation or acceptance of gifts; and (ii) provides refresher training on these topics to all travelers on the Europe trip as well as all staff involved in the planning and implementation of the trip.
>
> **Comments:** The Department has been inappropriately compelled and had an inadequate opportunity to review and respond to the Inspector General's report and the evidence that accompanied it. When the Department has completed its review the Deputy Secretary will in inform OIG as to whether it will accept this recommendation.

Appendix D

Appendix D

February 11, 2018, Response of the VA Secretary

By Email

The Honorable Michael J. Missal
Inspector General
Department of Veterans Affairs
801 I Street, N.W.
Washington, D.C. 20001

Justin V. Shur Molo Lamken LLP
600 New Hampshire Avenue, N.W.
Washington, D.C. 20037
T: 202.556.2005   F:
202.536.2015
jshur@mololamken.com
www.mololamken.com

February 11, 2018

Re: *Response to Administrative Investigation Draft Report:
VA Secretary and Delegation Travel to Europe*

Dear Mr. Missal:

We write in connection with your February 7, 2018 Draft Report concerning your Office's investigation into the VA Secretary's official travel to Europe in July 2017.

While we appreciate the important role of the Inspector General in protecting against fraud, waste, and abuse, we have grave concerns about your draft report. When you appeared before the House Appropriations Subcommittee on Military Construction, Veterans Affairs, and Related Agencies, you explained that VA OIG reports "must be accurate," "must be fair," and "must be objective." This report is none of those things.[54]

The draft report cannot be published in its current form. It ignores critical facts, presenting a one-sided version of events that casts aside evidence contradicting your chosen narrative. It improperly applies the relevant regulations, at times mischaracterizing them. And it imposes subjective and arbitrary criteria for evaluating the propriety of the Secretary's actions. Examples of our specific concerns are discussed further below.

The Hon. Michael Missal   - 2 -   February 11, 2018

---

[54] We understand information contained in this report has been leaked to *USA Today*. We are deeply troubled by this development. As you know, the report and its contents cannot be disclosed to anyone other than in connection with official review and comment. We trust that you will refer this serious breach of confidentiality to the Council of the Inspectors General on Integrity and Efficiency ("CIGIE") for investigation by an independent Inspector General.

I.   The Trip Was Immensely Valuable to the VA

As an initial matter, the report states that you were unable to determine the value of the trip to the VA. Draft Rpt. 19. Determining the value of the trip is, of course, outside your area of competence and expertise. It is the Secretary who is responsible for the care of the more than 20 million veterans in America. It is part of his job to continually learn about and actively participate in the developing issues facing veterans. As the Secretary explained in his voluntary interview, the trip was immensely valuable to his work and the VA's mission.

The Secretary was able to participate in hours of substantive meetings during his visit to Copenhagen, meeting with the Danish Ministry of Health to discuss the Danish healthcare system; participating in a roundtable discussion to discuss strategies for solutions to the population of aging veterans; and taking part in a question-and-answer session with the Danish Minister of Defense regarding veterans' policies. Likewise, the Five Eyes Ministerial Summit on Veterans' Affairs in London—which has regularly been attended by past VA Secretaries— was valuable given the Summit's focus on mental health issues facing veterans. Thus, it is obvious that the trip qualified as "essential" travel as described in the Secretary's June 29, 2017 Memorandum.

To suggest that the Secretary's participation in these conferences may not have been sufficiently valuable demonstrates a fundamental lack of understanding of the Secretary's work and the VA's mission. Secretary Shulkin did nothing wrong in traveling to Europe to meet with, and learn from, America's allies. Attending the conferences in Copenhagen and London was a valuable opportunity to strengthen the bond among allied countries whose retired soldiers are facing the same struggles as American veterans, and to engage in an idea and information exchange that will only improve veteran care on both sides of the Atlantic.

II.   Secretary Shulkin Did Not Improperly Accept Wimbledon Tickets

Your report notes that Secretary Shulkin, his wife, and his son attended Wimbledon as the guests of Victoria Gosling and her husband. They did so on the intervening Saturday between the meetings in Copenhagen and London. You suggest that the Secretary's acceptance of those tickets violated the federal gift regulations. Your analysis is highly flawed, both factually and legally. Most troubling is your repeated failure to disclose evidence that reveals the Secretary did nothing improper.[55] Ultimately, the Secretary violated no ethical regulations in accepting the tickets. That conclusion is supported by the attached expert declaration of Andrew D. Herman.

A.   The Tickets Were Not a Prohibited Gift

The federal gift regulations only prohibit government employees from accepting a gift from a "prohibited source"—someone who "[d]oes business or seeks to do business with the - 3 -

employee's agency"—or from someone who gave the gift because of the employee's official position. *See* 5 C.F.R. §§ 2635.201(a), 2635.202(b), 2635.203(d). Ms. Gosling is neither. Herman

---

[55] *See* Council for the Inspectors General on Integrity and Efficiency, *Quality Standards for Investigations* 14 (Nov. 15, 2011) ("CIGIE Quality Standards") (requiring that IG reports contain "exculpatory evidence and relevant mitigating information").

Decl. 19, 21. She made clear that she offered the Wimbledon tickets to the Secretary out of friendship and not because of his official position. *See, e.g.*, Gosling Decl. ¶¶ 14-15. Indeed, your office recognized that Ms. Gosling's statements during her interview "reflect [a] genuine friendliness and good will toward Secretary Shulkin and Dr. Bari." Draft Rpt. 14. Ms. Gosling, moreover, made clear that she would have offered the tickets to the Secretary even if he were not a government official. Gosling Decl. ¶ 15.

Ms. Gosling also is not a prohibited source. *See* Herman Decl. ¶ 19; 5 C.F.R. § 2635.203(d). You state that Sage Group—for whose charitable affiliate Ms. Gosling apparently works—holds contracts with various federal agencies. Your report does not mention, however, that the VA is **_not_** among them. Ms. Gosling did not do business with the VA, and she was not seeking to do business with the VA. Gosling Decl. ¶2. Neither did any employer of Ms. Gosling's. *Id.*[56] Notably, your report makes no finding to the contrary.[57]

Nonetheless, you state that the "prohibited source" requirement "would be another basis for the gift of the Wimbledon tickets to be improper." Draft Rpt. 16. That is wrong for two reasons. First, you make no finding that Ms. Gosling was a prohibited source. Herman Decl. ¶ 16. Second, your approach turns the proper legal analysis on its head. The conclusion that Ms. Gosling is a prohibited source is not "another basis" for finding the gift improper; it is, in fact, a **_threshold question_**. *Id.* ¶ 22. Your analysis fails at that threshold.

Because federal employees are prohibited only from accepting gifts from prohibited sources or gifts given because of their official position, and because you have not established that either occurred here, that should have been the beginning and the end of your analysis. Herman Decl. ¶ 22.

B. Section 2635.201(b) Does Not Prohibit Acceptance of the Tickets

Having failed to show that Secretary Shulkin was prohibited from accepting the tickets, you nonetheless insist that he acted improperly under 5 C.F.R. § 2635.201(b) because acceptance of the tickets would lead "a reasonable person [to] question [his] integrity or impartiality." Draft

---

[56] Your report states that Sage Foundation "has sought support from VA officials for its philanthropic initiatives supporting veterans," and identifies as the support an instance where then-Acting Deputy Secretary Scott Blackburn posed for a photo at a mental health event sponsored by Sage Foundation. Draft Rpt. 9 n.20. You do not appear to have interviewed Mr. Blackburn or to have asked him about this event. Had you done so, you would have learned from Mr. Blackburn that the VA offered no financial support to Sage Foundation for that event.

[57] However, you state—without identifying *any* supporting evidence—that "[b]y virtue of her business relationships, . . . Ms. Gosling may also meet the definition of a 'prohibited source.' " Draft Rpt. 16 (emphasis added). That sort of innuendo—unsupported by any reasoned analysis and evidence, and falling well short of an affirmative finding— has no place in an objective, impartial, and unbiased report. Indeed, CIGIE's Quality Standards caution that "conjecture [or] unsubstantiated opinion" should play no role in an investigative report. Your prohibited source analysis cannot be reconciled with that admonition. If your investigation could not substantiate the allegation that Ms. Gosling was a prohibited source, your report should say so. It should not assert without any factual basis that Ms. Gosling "may" have been one.

Rpt. 15; *see also* 5 C.F.R. §2635.201. You neglect to mention, however, that §2635.201(b) is a "*non-binding* standard,"[58] that applies only to the acceptance of "an otherwise *permissible* gift []," 5 C.F.R. §2635.201(b) (emphasis added). Herman Decl. ¶¶24-25. Your suggestion that this hortatory regulation applies thus admits that the Secretary was legally entitled to accept the tickets.

Moreover, your office is without authority to opine on the applicability of § 2635.201(b). As the Office of Government Ethics ("OGE") has explained, "[§ 2635.201(b)] does not change the fact that *the determination as to whether a legally permissible gift should be accepted is the employee's to make*." 81 Fed. Reg. at 81,642. (emphasis added); *see also* Herman Decl. ¶¶ 2, 5. Your report's failure to disclose any of this simply underscores its lack of objectivity and its bias.

Regardless, § 2635.201(b) does not apply here. You accurately identify the four factors relevant to an analysis under that provision, but you provide no meaningful analysis of how those factors apply here. Draft Rpt. 15. Indeed, you discuss only one of those four factors—the value of the gift. The Wimbledon tickets were no doubt valuable, but not as valuable as you say. Your report improperly relies upon the value of the tickets on the secondary market to suggest that the tickets were worth thousands more than their actual value. *See* Herman Decl. 28-29.

In particular, you note that the "lowest asking price" for tickets to the 2018 Ladies' Finals at Wimbledon on unspecified "commercial websites" was £1,205.00 (approximately $1,760), and you suggest that the cost of attending the 2017 match would have been comparable. Draft Rpt. 9 n.19.[59] But the face value of the tickets that Secretary Shulkin and his wife received was £155 each, and the ticket for their son cost £34.[60] The exchange rate for U.S. dollars to pounds sterling on July 15, 2017 was 1.3. Thus, the total value of the tickets that Ms. Gosling provided was approximately $450—well below the $3,500 value suggested in your report.

Moreover, the other factors—the one's you do not discuss—weigh heavily in the Secretary's favor. *See* Herman Decl. ¶¶ 30-32. For example, nothing about "the timing of the gift creates the appearance that the donor is seeking to influence an official action." 5 C.F.R. §2635.201(b)(2)(ii); Herman Decl. ¶ 30. You identify no official action whatsoever that Ms. Gosling's gift was intended to influence. Nor do you assert that Ms. Gosling is "a person who

---

[58] Standards of Ethical Conduct for Employees of the Executive Branch; Amendment to the Standards Governing Solicitation and Acceptance of Gifts from Outside Sources, 81 Fed. Reg. 81,641, 81,641 (Nov. 18, 2016) (emphasis added).

[59] Stating that you were "not able to determine the availability and cost of 2017 Wimbledon tickets on commercial websites after the tournament concluded," you instead rely on the secondary market value of tickets to the 2018 Wimbledon tournament. However, you could have determined this information simply by accessing Wimbledon's website, which when accessed two days ago still listed 2017 ticket prices. *See* Tickets and Ticket Prices, 2017 Tickets, https://www.wimbledon.com/en_GB/atoz/tickets_and_ticket_prices.html (last accessed Feb. 9, 2018).

[60] OGE has made clear that the value of ticketed events is the face value of the ticket, not any inflated value the tickets may have on the secondary market. *See* Legal Advisory to Designated Agency Ethics Officials Presidential Inaugural Events, OGE Informal Advisory Letter LA-16-11, 2016 WL 7404631, at *1 (Dec. 20, 2016); Standards of Ethical Conduct for Employees of the Executive Branch, 57 Fed. Reg. 35,006-01 (Aug. 7, 1992) (rejecting argument that tickets be valued at higher than face value).

has interests that may be substantially affected by the performance or nonperformance of" the -
5 -

Secretary's official duties. 5 C.F.R. § 2635.201(b)(2)(iii); Herman Decl. ¶¶ 20-21, 31. And nothing about the tickets provided Ms. Gosling with "significantly disproportionate access." 5 C.F.R. § 2635.201(b)(2)(iv); Herman Decl. ¶ 32. In short, while you emphasize that all four factors "must [be] consider[ed]," Draft Rpt. 15 n.29, you in fact only consider one—the value of the gift, making that factor outcome-determinative. If OGE intended that to be the analysis, it would simply have prohibited federal employees from accepting gifts over a certain value.

Ultimately, you have no authority to second-guess an employee's decision to not decline a permissible gift under the non-binding and hortatory standard of §2635.201(b). In any event, your insufficient analysis involving one of the four appropriate factors simply underscores that § 2635.201(b) did not counsel rejection of the gift here.

C. The Personal Friendship Exception Is Irrelevant

Your conclusion that the Secretary should not have accepted the Wimbledon tickets is based on the "personal friendship" exception under the gift rules. But that exception is only relevant if the tickets were a prohibited gift (*e.g.*, if Ms. Gosling was a "prohibited source"). As discussed above, the tickets were not a prohibited gift and thus the personal friendship exception is irrelevant. Herman Decl. ¶ 22. In any event, your application of the personal friendship exception, though legally irrelevant, is deeply flawed. And, most problematically, it rests largely on evidence and testimony that was procured through your investigator's misconduct and improper questioning.

> 1. *The Personal Friendship Exception Would Justify Acceptance of the Tickets*

You have concluded that the personal friendship exception does not permit acceptance of the tickets because, in your view, Ms. Gosling and the Secretary's wife are not in sufficiently close contact—that they did not email or text frequently enough to meet your standard of friendship. Draft Rpt. 13-15. The "closeness" of the friendship is not the standard. Rather, the exception applies so long as the gift is given "under circumstances which make it clear that the gift *is motivated by* a . . . personal friendship." 5 C.F.R. § 2635.204(b) (emphasis added). The exception is not limited to situations where the friends are "close." So long as the gift is motivated by the friendship—whatever the strength of the bond—the exception applies.

Here, it is clear that Ms. Gosling's gift of the Wimbledon tickets was motivated by her personal relationship with Dr. Bari and the Secretary. Ms. Gosling told you that herself when you interviewed her. As she explained, "I enjoy [the Secretary's] company. I enjoy his wife's company. . . . I really got on very well with his wife." Draft Rpt. 16. And Ms. Gosling reiterated those sentiments in her declaration. Gosling Decl. ¶¶3-5, 7, 9, 13-14. The Secretary, moreover, explained during his interview that Ms. Gosling and his wife were friends. And you do not dispute that Dr. Bari and Ms. Gosling were friendly on three separate occasions when Ms. Gosling had traveled to the United States: at events hosted by the British Embassy, the Invictus Games, and the Canadian Embassy. *Id.* ¶¶ 3-5, 7; Draft Rpt. 9. At these events, Ms. Gosling and

6 -   February 11, 2018 Dr. Bari chatted and enjoyed each other's company in a purely social context. *Id.* [61] (It was the Secretary—not his wife—who attended these functions as a government official and who had official duties to perform.) You also decry what you perceive to be the lack of emails, text messages, and phone records between Dr. Bari and Ms. Gosling, as if the quality of a friendship can be measured in emojis. But you wholly ignore the substance of the communications that you did receive:

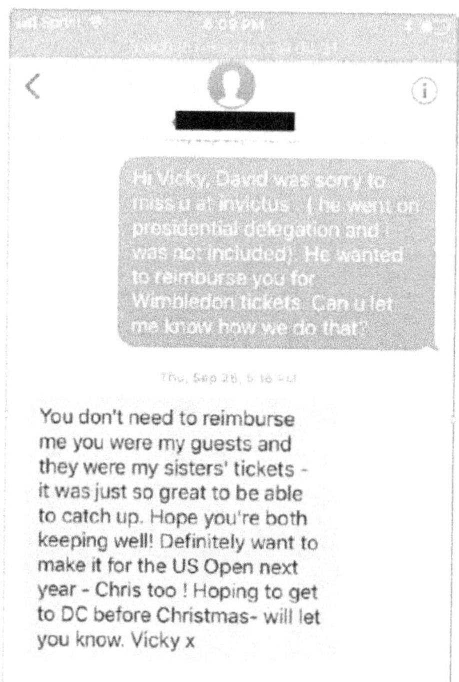

Those are not the communications of business associates with a purely professional relationship. Indeed, few co-workers sign their emails with "kisses."[62] Your failure to reveal the substance of this text exchange in your report and acknowledge that it supports a showing of friendship between Ms. Gosling and Dr. Bari simply underscores that your office did not approach this investigation in an objective and unbiased manner.[63]

---

[61] You characterize these interactions as "brief [ ]." Draft Rpt. 13. That is pure conjecture. You cite no evidence and invoke no testimony establishing the length of Ms. Gosling's and Dr. Bari's interactions, and your finding on this point is highly improper. *See* CIGIE Quality Standards, at 11. Ms. Gosling, moreover, described the interactions differently, saying that she spoke with Dr. Bari at length during these events. Gosling Decl. ¶ 7.

[62] *See* Nadine Epstein, *A Whole Lot of History Behind 'X' and 'O,' Kiss and Hug*, The Wash. Post (Feb. 13, 2014), https://www.washingtonpost.com/lifestyle/style/a-whole-lot-of-history-behind-x-and-o-kiss-and-hug/2014/02/13/0c3e218a-9341-11e3-b46a-5a3d0d2130da_story.html?utm_term=.c852bb1171e3.

[63] Your report also fails to acknowledge that the Secretary repeatedly offered—both before Wimbledon and after— to pay Ms. Gosling for the tickets. Instead, you suggest that the Secretary only offered to pay for the tickets after *The Washington Post* inquired about them. But you ignore the Secretary's testimony—and supporting email—that he repeatedly offered to pay Ms. Gosling for the tickets prior to that. For example, on July 4, 2017, the Secretary wrote Ms. Gosling, "Yes it would be great to be able to use your sister's tickets . . . just let me know how much I

You similarly fail to acknowledge that Ms. Gosling's own statements "corroborate the purported closeness of the relationship over several years." Ms. Gosling told you—twice—about her friendship with Dr. Bari and the Secretary. Indeed, you admit that Ms. Gosling's statements "reflect genuine friendliness and good will" toward the Secretary and his wife. Draft Rpt. 14; *see also* Gosling Decl. ¶¶ 3-5, 7, 9, 13-14. If that is not corroboration, nothing is.

Finally, you suggest that an example in the rule establishing the personal friendship exception supports your conclusion that the exception does not apply to the Wimbledon tickets. However, you misrepresent the example.

According to your account, the example involves a government employee who met an individual at an official meeting. The two thereafter "communicated occasionally." Draft Rpt. 15. That is not accurate. The example actually states that the "two communicated occasionally ***regarding contract matters***" and "***did not*** communicate further in their personal capacities, carry on extensive personal interactions, or meet socially outside of work." 5 C.F.R. § 2635.204(b) (emphasis added). That makes all the difference: The example makes clear that, aside from connecting on social media, ***all interactions*** between the two individuals were work-related. That does not describe the relationship between the Secretary's wife and Ms. Gosling. To the contrary, Dr. Bari and Ms. Gosling did communicate in their personal capacities, did have personal interactions, and did meet socially. That Dr. Bari and Ms. Gosling met at events attended by the Secretary as a government official does not make the interactions between Dr. Bari and Ms. Gosling any less social. Indeed, their topics of conversation related to tennis and other personal matters, not having anything to do with business. Gosling Decl. ¶¶ 3-5, 7.

2.   *Your Report Relies on Evidence Adduced Through Investigative Misconduct*

Most problematic about your personal friendship analysis, however, is the extent to which you rely on evidence gathered through highly improper, highly suggestive, and highly unreliable questioning techniques. Your report acknowledges that, after the trip, Ethics Counsel reviewed the Secretary's acceptance of the Wimbledon tickets and determined acceptance of the gift was proper.[11]

You now dismiss the opinion that Ethics Counsel rendered. According to your report, Ethics Counsel has now reversed that opinion based on "additional information" that your investigators provided her. Because it is unclear from your report what additional information you provided to Ethics Counsel, we requested a copy of the transcript of your interview of her. The portion of the transcript we received clearly reveals the questioning that yielded the "revised opinion" was highly improper and highly suggestive. It involved long narrative expositions from

---

owe you." Your report makes no mention of this correspondence. And if your investigators asked Ms. Gosling whether the Secretary ever offered to pay for the tickets, her response is not mentioned in your report.

[11] Your report appears critical of the fact that Ethics Counsel did not review acceptance of the Wimbledon tickets until after the trip. *See* Draft Rpt. v, 11-13 & n.25. During Secretary Shulkin's interview, however, your office commended the Secretary for seeking out such review: A representative of your office told the Secretary that he "appreciate[d] the fact that" Secretary Shulkin "initiated that" ethics review. "That was good," he said.

██████████████████████████ not only describing evidence for the witness, but also providing ████████ own conclusions about what the evidence meant and how, in his view, it demonstrated the impropriety of the Secretary's actions. For example, after showing Ethics Counsel an email from the Secretary to Ms. Gosling, in which the Secretary referred to "my wife" and "my son," ████████ said:

> I mean, in my world as an investigator, I pick up on nuances like that, that's what I'm trained to do—to, to kind of get to where I need to go. And, um, that was a clear indicator to me that the relationship that [the Secretary] described between his wife and Vicky Gosling, uh, was much different here in this June 25th email than it was in the September 28th email. He's referring to her, you know, as my wife, when if they're good friends, he, he should—he would've said Merle. I mean that's just—that's just the—that's very common, and it's almost beyond reasonable doubt, 99 percent of the time, people would say if, if they were that good of friends, as he described here, they're going to—he's going to say Merle. He's not going to say my wife.

> And that's, again, it's, it's, it's not the end-all, the be-all. You know, it's not the whole—it's not like, okay, that, that proves something. Uh, it just—it, it, it's, it's very, very telling.

> * * *

> Well, a husband referring to his wife in that sense as a her or a she is very significant and is very telling because it's, it's out of place. It just—it's, it's, uh—it's very—it, it tells you—it tells me, a trained investigator, that there's something wrong with the relationship. Now, it may not be—it may not be long—a long term problem, but it could be that they had a fight that morning, (laughter), or there's some riff, there's something going on there.

> We also see it when—where he's [the Secretary] talking about in the third party sense where he's, you know—he can't—he can't tell Vicky Gosling the name of his wife because really, they're not friends. And that's the idea behind, behind how, how we look at that. Again, it's not totality proof or anything, it's just in, in the big context of things.

Unsurprisingly, when ████████ next asked Ethics Counsel if that email changed her opinion, she responded that it did.

████████ improper questioning continued. For over *fifteen pages of transcript* from Ethics Counsel's interview (pp. 86:17 through 101:13), ████████ described in great depth the evidence and information that he believed demonstrated that the Secretary had acted improperly. He provided the witness with his own conclusions from that evidence. And perhaps most troubling, ████████ downplays and dismisses evidence that favors the Secretary.

As demonstrated by the transcript, ████████ questioning runs far afield of CIGIE's Quality Standards for Investigations, which admonish investigators that "[e]vidence must be gathered . . . in an unbiased and independent manner." CIGIE Quality Standards, at 8. Indeed, authorities across the country have recognized that suggestive questioning such as that employed by ███████ is not only improper, but uniquely unsuited for uncovering the truth. Experts in this area have found that questions where an interviewer provides his own opinion are particularly inappropriate and should be avoided.[12] Given ███████ employed these improper techniques when questioning Ethics Counsel, her responses simply cannot be trusted. They carry little weight, if any at all.

While ███████ went to great lengths to describe and characterize for Ethics Counsel evidence that he believed showed the Secretary acted improperly, ███████ neglected to provide Ethics Counsel with additional information that supported the Secretary's acceptance of the gift. ███████ apparently did not provide Ethics Counsel with the text message exchange between Dr. Bari and Ms. Gosling, or Ms. Gosling's statements that "[Secretary Shulkin] and his wife are friends of mine," or with your own finding that Ms. Gosling exhibited "genuine friendliness" toward the Secretary and his wife when you interviewed her. Draft Rpt. 14. ███████ also did not ask Ethics Counsel to opine on whether Ms. Gosling was a prohibited source. Nor did he ask Ethics Counsel to balance the four § 2635.201(b) factors. These facts and issues are all critical to the ethics analysis and all support the Secretary's acceptance of the tickets, yet ███████ does not appear to have given Ethics Counsel an opportunity to consider them.

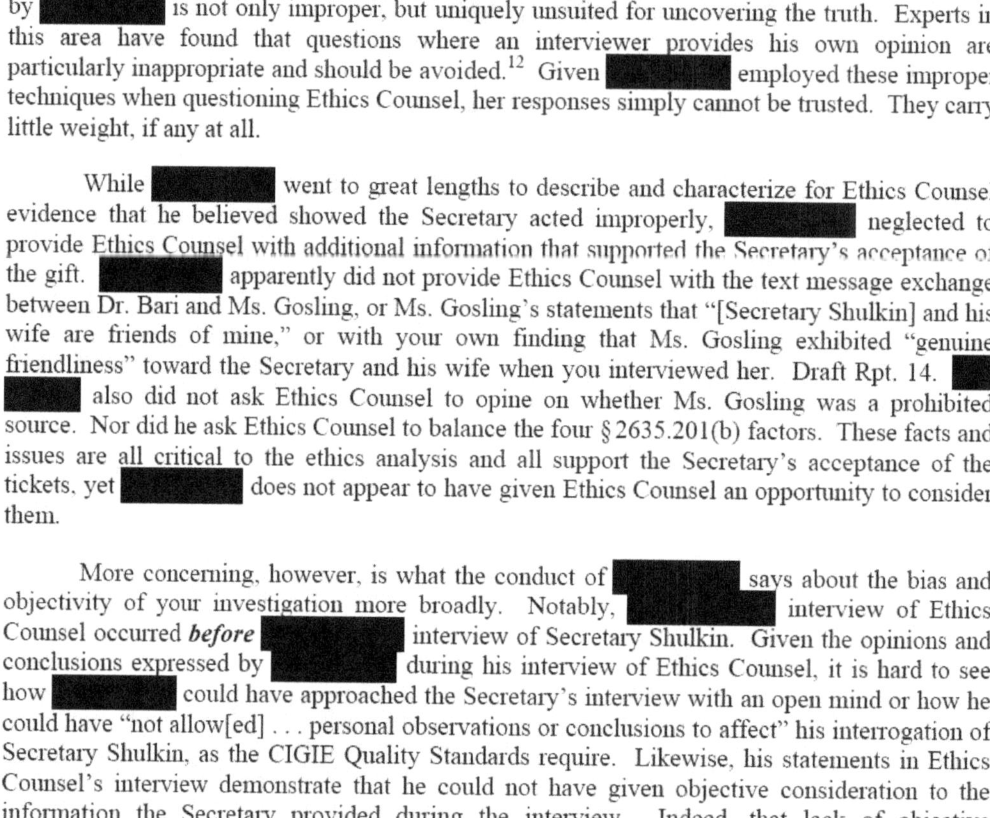

More concerning, however, is what the conduct of ███████ says about the bias and objectivity of your investigation more broadly. Notably, ███████ interview of Ethics Counsel occurred *before* ███████ interview of Secretary Shulkin. Given the opinions and conclusions expressed by ███████ during his interview of Ethics Counsel, it is hard to see how ███████ could have approached the Secretary's interview with an open mind or how he could have "not allow[ed] . . . personal observations or conclusions to affect" his interrogation of Secretary Shulkin, as the CIGIE Quality Standards require. Likewise, his statements in Ethics Counsel's interview demonstrate that he could not have given objective consideration to the information the Secretary provided during the interview. Indeed, that lack of objective consideration is apparent from the face of your report, which repeatedly demands external corroboration of any information provided by the Secretary—even in the absence of any reason to distrust what the Secretary has said—but accepts as gospel the testimony of other individuals that ███████ interviewed.

As you know, when we left Secretary Shulkin's interview, we were seriously troubled by the conduct of ███████ who led the questioning. We raised these concerns in a letter to your Counselor, Christopher Wilber. Our review of excerpts from the transcript of ███████ interview of Ethics Counsel has only amplified our concerns and calls into question the credibility and validity of all other testimony quoted in your draft report. We request the entire transcripts of all interviews conducted in this investigation. If ███████ or other investigators, have conducted those interviews in the same manner that ███████ interviewed the Secretary and Ethics Counsel, there is very little to trust in your report.

---

[12] *See, e.g.*, Gavin E. Oxburgh *et al.*, *The Question of Question Types in Police Interviews: A Review of the Literature from a Psychological and Linguistic Perspective*, 17 The Int'l J. of Speech, Language, & the Law 46, 60 (2010).

- 10 -

In any event, the "additional information" that, according to you, prompted Ethics Counsel to reverse her determination does not support the conclusion that the Secretary should not have accepted the Wimbledon tickets. Draft Rpt. 14. You say that additional information included: (1) "emails indicating that Ms. Gosling was seeking an introduction to Secretary Shulkin through an intermediary," and (2) emails in which "Ms. Gosling requested Secretary Shulkin's assistance in gaining an invitation to the London Summit." *Id.* The intermediary's emails do nothing to undermine the Ethics Counsel's initial conclusion that acceptance of the tickets was proper. They convey pure hearsay, and there is good reason to doubt the credibility of the author. It simply makes no sense that Ms. Gosling would request an introduction to Secretary Shulkin when she had met him three times prior. *Id.* at 9. Glaringly, when your investigators interviewed Ms. Gosling, they apparently never asked her about this topic, once again refusing to seek out information that might explain or mitigate suspicions that the investigators harbored. Had they done so, they would have learned that Ms. Gosling did not, in fact, ask for an introduction to the Secretary in 2017. Gosling Decl. ¶ 6. Nor does Ms. Gosling's request for assistance in securing an invitation to the Summit alter the outcome of the analysis. Ms. Gosling obtained that invitation from other sources and, as the Secretary told you, he did nothing to help Ms. Gosling obtain an invitation to the Summit.

We are also concerned that the Executive Summary prominently featured the fact that Ms. Gosling could not remember Dr. Bari's first name when you interviewed her. Draft Rpt. iv, 16 n.33. Its prominence in the Executive Summary seems designed to make headlines, not objectively report the facts. That you relegate this fact to a footnote in your analysis— demonstrating that Ms. Gosling's memory lapse is relatively unimportant—illustrates this point.

In any event, Ms. Gosling attributed her memory lapse to a mental block and to the conduct of your investigators when they interviewed her. Gosling Decl. ¶ 8.[64] Your emphasis on that memory lapse makes something out of nothing. Such mental blocks happen all the time. History abounds with examples of people momentarily and embarrassingly forgetting information that they obviously know. The Chief Justice, for example, famously forgot the Oath of Office during President Obama's 2009 Inauguration.[65] And Canada's Prime Minister, Justin Trudeau, embarrassingly forgot to mention Alberta when listing all of Canada's provinces during a

---

[64] Ms. Gosling's account of her interview seems particularly credible given your harassment in trying to secure the interview (attempting to contact Ms. Gosling 22 times over the course of seven weeks, Draft Rpt. 16 & n.33) and your investigators' conduct in the interviews of Secretary Shulkin and Ethics Counsel.

[65] Jeff Zeleny, *I Really Do Swear, Faithfully: Obama and Roberts Try Again*, The N.Y. Times (Jan. 21, 2009), http://www.nytimes.com/2009/01/22/us/politics/22oath.html.

speech.[66] And neither the Chief Justice nor the Prime Minister, when their memories failed, faced the rigors of strenuous questioning by adversarial investigators.

Ultimately, Ms. Gosling had no business before the VA. Ms. Gosling and Secretary Shulkin's wife were friends—as Ms. Gosling herself told you. Under those circumstances, there was nothing improper about the Secretary's acceptance of the Wimbledon tickets.

- 11 -

III.   The Secretary's Statements to the Media Were Not Misleading

You accuse the VA—and the Secretary—of making misleading statements to *The Washington Post*. Nothing about the Secretary's statements was misleading. On November 9, 2017, Secretary Shulkin sat for a nearly hour-long interview with *The Washington Post*'s Ed O'Keefe. They discussed many of the most pressing issues facing veterans today, including veterans' mental health and improvements in VA care.

Mr. O'Keefe also raised the Secretary's trip to Europe, asking whether the Secretary bought the Wimbledon tickets. According to your report, the Secretary responded, "Yes, they were privately done, no government money." You interpret the Secretary's response as indicating that he had purchased the tickets himself, which you believe is misleading. As the Secretary explained during his interview with your agents, however, his initial response to the question— "yes"—was not a substantive response to the question but an affirmative indication that he would be happy to address that issue. Inexplicably, your report does not mention the Secretary's explanation for his answer to this question. And the substantive response the Secretary gave—that the Wimbledon tickets were "privately done" with "no government money"—was entirely accurate.

You further suggest that the Secretary was misleading when he responded to Mr. O'Keefe's question about whether the Wimbledon tickets were a gift from "folks at the Invictus Games." Draft Rpt. 23-24. Your agents never asked the Secretary about this response during his interview, and your office has not until now raised any concerns about the Secretary's response to this question. Had these concerns been raised, the Secretary would have explained that his answer was entirely truthful. When Ms. Gosling offered the tickets, she was no longer the CEO of the Invictus games, instead holding a role as an unpaid strategic advisor to the UK delegation. And she in fact purchased the tickets (for her sister, initially) with her own money. Gosling Decl. ¶ 10. The cost of the tickets was not paid for or reimbursed by the Invictus Foundation.

Finally, you suggest that the VA press office issued a misleading statement to *The Washington Post* on September 29, 2017. Specifically, you take issue with the statement that "all activities including Wimbledon were reviewed and approved by Ethics Counsel." As Secretary Shulkin

---

[66] Avi Selk, *'We Already Know You Hate Alberta': How Justin Trudeau Managed To Insult an Entire Province*, The Wash. Post (July 2, 2017), https://www.washingtonpost.com/news/worldviews/w.p/2017/07/02/we-already-knowyou-hate-alberta-how-justin-trudeau-managed-to-insult-an-entire-province/?utm_term=.7a680384a8d7

explained in his interview, he had nothing to do with the drafting of that statement.[67]   The statement, moreover, was true with respect to the Wimbledon tickets—when the VA press secretary emailed that statement to *The Washington Post* around noon on September 29, 2017, Ethics Counsel had reviewed and approved the Wimbledon tickets.

Moreover, to the extent the statement could have been drafted more clearly, it is apparent that the statement was the result of haste, not an intentional effort to mislead. Jim Byrne, the VA's General Counsel, for example, explained that he reviewed the statement for "about 20 seconds" before clearing its release. And the VA press secretary's statements to *The Washington* - 12 -

Post included inaccuracies that, if corrected, would have benefitted the Secretary. For example, the VA press secretary told *The Post* that Dr. Bari's "[m]eals and incidentals were covered under per diem." That was not true: Dr. Bari never received a per diem or reimbursement for meals and incidentals. Your report does not discuss these inaccuracies, which seriously undermine your suggestion that the VA and the Secretary engaged in a campaign to mislead the media.

Your accusation that the Secretary misled *The Washington Post* is particularly puzzling, given the Secretary's open and professed commitment to transparency. Indeed, Secretary Shulkin has taken the extreme action of posting on the VA website details regarding all his travel, including the means of transportation and the composition of the delegation. No other agency has been so transparent. And, even beyond the topic of his official travel, the Secretary has worked hard to make sure that all components of the VA are held to the highest standards of transparency to ensure accountability and guarantee that the civil servants who serve America's veterans are the best in government.

IV. Secretary Shulkin Reasonably Relied on Approval from VA Ethics Officials Concerning His Wife's Travel at Government Expense

Dr. Bari accompanied Secretary Shulkin—as spouses of cabinet members often do—as an invited guest to the conferences in both Copenhagen and London. Indeed, other spouses or significant others of the Secretary's foreign counterparts were present at the London conference, too. Your report, however, takes issue with the fact that the VA paid for Dr. Bari's coach-class airfare to and from Europe.

Dr. Bari's invitational travel, however, was approved by Ethics Counsel. You question the validity of that approval because you allege that the VA Chief of Staff altered emails in order to obtain that approval. The Secretary had **nothing** to do with the process of obtaining approval for his wife's official travel. In fact, Secretary Shulkin and Dr. Bari were prepared to pay for Dr. Bari's travel as they had always done previously. It was only when staff approached the Secretary

---

[67] You suggest the Secretary's testimony on this point conflicts with the testimony of John Ullyot, the VA's Assistant Secretary for Public and Intergovernmental Affairs. But your report gives no reason to credit Mr. Ullyot's testimony over the Secretary's, and you make no specific finding regarding the Secretary's participation in the drafting of the press statement.

to suggest Dr. Bari's travel could be reimbursed that Secretary Shulkin became aware that was a possibility.[68] He neither was aware of nor approved any communications between his staff and Ethics Counsel. Your report, however, does not make that clear. Regardless, when Secretary Shulkin learned through his staff that Dr. Bari's invitational travel had been approved by Ethics Counsel, he was entitled to rely on that approval—regardless of your allegations of impropriety arising from emails that the Secretary never saw and never approved.

- 13 -

V. The Secretary Was Not Involved In or Aware of VA's Travel Documentation for the Europe Trip

Your report suggests that the VA delegation provided inadequate documentation to determine the appropriateness of certain travel expenses. Your analysis is incomplete and raises concerns better addressed by the VA at large rather than directed at the Secretary.

Secretary Shulkin was not involved in coordinating travel for the delegation or otherwise planning the day-to-day travel arrangements for the official trip. These tasks were rightfully delegated to his staff. That is not unusual. The Secretary's reliance upon his staff for travel coordination and submission of paperwork is particularly appropriate, given that the Travel Office staff is well versed in the applicable rules and regulations, and this trip concerned travel for other members of the VA. Secretary Shulkin did nothing wrong in relying on his staff to submit and prepare such paperwork. Indeed, your office might appropriately be concerned if the Secretary were spending his time completing administrative paperwork rather than focusing on the important work of improving the healthcare and benefits that America provides its veterans.

VI. The Secretary Did Not Improperly Direct the Misuse of Official Time and Did Not Violate Any Regulations by Touring Cultural Sites

You accuse the Secretary and his wife of inappropriately requiring VA Program Specialist Gabe Gough to assist in planning visits for the delegation to tourist and cultural sites. According to your report, "Secretary Shulkin directed [Mr. Gough] to coordinate with his wife to schedule the tourist activities that they wanted to do on nonofficial time." Draft Rpt. 17.

Your report ignores, however, that Mr. Gough began planning those tourist activities before Secretary Shulkin told him to do anything. On June 23, 2017, Mr. Gough emailed the Secretary: "Sir, I wanted to run what we've been planning for the London section of the trip by you." Mr.

---

[68] Your report states that, according to VA employee Gabe Gough, the Secretary asked if VA could pay his wife's expenses. The Secretary made no such request. As the Secretary explained during his interview, until his staff informed him that VA could pay his wife's expenses as an invitational traveler, the Secretary's wife had planned to pay for her own airfare. Draft Rpt. 4. You note that your office did not need to resolve the conflicting memories between the Secretary and Mr. Gough. *Id.* at 4 n.11. Your report, however, does precisely that: "The OIG found that after Secretary Shulkin asked in April 2017 if VA could pay for his wife's travel expenses . . . ." *Id.* at ii. Regardless, even by Mr. Gough's account, the Secretary acted appropriately by relying on the approval of Ethics Counsel.

Gough goes on to explain that the delegation can purchase a "London Pass" to "cover all entry fees" at the various tourist sites. And Mr. Gough says he had "thought about a trip to Stonehenge, but it's 2 hours away." Mr. Gough concludes by inviting the Secretary and Dr. Bari to let him know if they are interested in any sites or restaurants that he has not already included in the itinerary. Thus, Mr. Gough **on his own initiative** undertook the detailed planning of tourist activities. Only when Mr. Gough approached the Secretary with this information did the Secretary refer Mr. Gough to Dr. Bari. And, as the Secretary explained in his interview, he referred Mr. Gough to his wife only because, as you might expect, he was too busy to be concerned with the details of planning tourist activities. Your failure to disclose that it was Mr. Gough who initiated the detailed planning of tourist activities, and that it was Mr. Gough who approached the Secretary, is troubling. It presents yet another example of your willingness to cherry-pick facts that support your sensationalist narrative rather than objectively report what happened.

Regardless, Mr. Gough had good reason to be involved in planning the non-official events during the trip. As he told you himself, his involvement was necessary to coordinate security coverage for Secretary Shulkin. Draft Rpt. 17. That effort involved coordination not just with the Secretary's security detail, but also with officials at the American Embassies in London and Copenhagen. Indeed, it was security—through Mr. Gough—that suggested the - 14 -

delegation purchase the London and Copenhagen passes. You suggest that Mr. Gough's "planning efforts" went beyond those required to coordinate security, saying that he could have done so "without engaging in the extensive research and planning tasks." Draft Rpt. 18. But as we explained, Mr. Gough initiated those planning efforts on his own.

Dr. Bari, moreover, engaged in her own planning. For example, she reached out to her own contacts in London to identify potential tourist sites. And she researched on her own restaurants and sites to visit both in London and Copenhagen. To the extent Dr. Bari relied upon Mr. Gough to schedule visits and generate an itinerary, she did so because any non-official activities had to be coordinated with official activities, VA events, and the schedules of the other members of the delegation. It would have been improper and unrealistic for Dr. Bari to engage in the necessary communications with VA personnel, the security detail, and diplomatic staff in order to undertake all that planning herself.

Your report also appears to criticize the Secretary for attending any tourist activities at all. Your criticisms are both misplaced and unreasonable. As an initial matter, the color-coded calendar purporting to show "Scheduled official business" and "Scheduled leisure" is false and misleading. *See* Draft Rpt. ii. You have labeled Tuesday, July 11 a "Day in Transit." But, until he left for the airport that afternoon, the Secretary spent the day treating patients at the New York VA. July 11 was thus a workday. Your calendar also suggests that the delegation scheduled leisure for half the day on Thursday, July 13. In reality, the delegation attended official events through 2:30 p.m., and then resumed official events later that evening for an official dinner hosted by the American Embassy. Your report should reflect the official nature of those events.

Finally, your report fails to designate Saturday, July 15—the day the Secretary traveled from Copenhagen to London—as a "Day in Transit."[69]

Your calendar also does not take account of the fact that, during the periods you have labeled "Scheduled leisure," the Secretary was working. Even as the delegation was touring cultural sites, the Secretary was taking phone calls, answering emails, and tending to VA business. He even gave a radio interview during this time. You acknowledge that the Secretary told investigators about those efforts during his interview, yet you stop short of making a finding that the Secretary did in fact work throughout the trip. Draft Rpt. 1. That too evinces an unwillingness to accept the Secretary's testimony even when it goes unchallenged and even when you could easily have corroborated it. For example, you reviewed over 12,000 documents and searched 493,000 emails. Surely, those documents included evidence of the Secretary's efforts on behalf of the VA while overseas, but you do not mention them. You interviewed 28 individuals in connection with this investigation, including the Secretary's six-member security staff and other members of the delegation. You could have asked them about the Secretary's efforts, but apparently did not. Your investigators' failure to do so is yet one more instance of them seeking out information to further their chosen narrative while suppressing or ignoring information that bolsters the Secretary's testimony.

- 15 -

More fundamentally, there was nothing improper about the Secretary taking time to tour sites of historical and cultural significance while in London and Copenhagen. VA travel policy expressly permits employees to combine official travel with personal travel. *See* VA Travel Admin. Guide 9-10. And, as you might expect, the Secretary's hours of work are not limited to the standard nine-to-five workday. Indeed, the Secretary is exempt from the typical annual- and sick-leave rules, meaning he can take vacation only as the demands of his job allow. *See* 5 C.F.R. § 630.211(a)(3). (Rest assured, the Secretary's "vacations"—to the extent they can be called that, given how much he works during those times—are few and far between.)[70]

Nor was it improper for the Secretary to remain in Europe between the two conferences. Indeed, the travel regulations would have allowed the delegation to return to the U.S. only if "substantial cost savings" resulted. 41 C.F.R. § 301-11.23(b). You make no effort to show that flying the entire VA delegation to the U.S. from Copenhagen, only to return to London two days later, would have yielded such savings.

In any event, your report—and its misleading calendar—does not adequately represent the number of hours Secretary Shulkin spent on official business. As explained during the Secretary's

---

[69] We have attached to this letter a calendar that more accurately reflects the Secretary's approximate use of his time during the trip.

[70] Your report also mentions shopping in Copenhagen and Malmo, Sweden (only a 30-minute train ride from Copenhagen). The Secretary and his wife, however, bought nothing on the trip, except perhaps a few souvenirs for VA staff.

interview, the vast majority of his time in Copenhagen and London was spent on official duties.[71] Any sightseeing by the Secretary was incidental to the substance of the trip.

*   *   *

We left the Secretary's interview on December 14 with grave concerns about the objectivity and the fairness with which your office was pursuing this investigation. As we explained in our December 21 letter, the conduct of the investigators who interviewed the Secretary left us worried that those investigators were intent on portraying the Secretary unfavorably and were not impartially obtaining and evaluating the facts. Your Counselor, Mr. Wilber, responded that "it is the policy of OIG to review the facts and evidence collected in any matter . . . objectively and fairly." He assured us that your office "will do so here." That promise appears to have gone unfulfilled.

As we have explained above, your report presents a one-sided account of the circumstances surrounding the Secretary's trip to Europe. It omits critical facts and pieces of evidence that contradict your chosen narrative and that make clear the Secretary has done nothing wrong. Indeed, it seems obvious that your investigators have failed in some instances to even pursue such evidence. And your investigators have relied on interrogation techniques that have long since been recognized as unfair, unreliable, and abusive. Your report, moreover, confuses and misapplies legal standards in an effort to manufacture violations where none exist.

- 16 -

Even after you provided us with a copy of your draft report, your office's tactics seem intentionally designed to prevent a full airing of the facts and circumstances underlying the trip. For example, your staff provided a draft copy of the report very late in the evening on Monday, February 5, and on February 7, provided us a revised draft that included information from a recently conducted interview of a key witness. Nonetheless, you set a February 9 deadline for submitting a response. Thus, where standard OIG practice appears to allow up to 30 days for a response, you initially afforded us less than five days. And, although your staff acknowledged that no external pressures mandated the tight turn-around for our response, our request for more time was met with an extension of less than 48 hours, setting the deadline at 6:00 p.m. on Sunday, February 11.

Given the serious nature of the issues raised herein, your draft report cannot be published in its current form. Substantial revisions are needed to ensure that the report accurately describes the events in question and conveys findings that are appropriately supported by the facts. We trust that after reviewing this submission you will reach the same conclusion. However, if you do not and decide to publish your report without addressing all the problems we identified, we demand

---

[71] Your report notes that during the trip there was a "crisis" unfolding at the Manchester VA. Draft Rpt. 19 n.34. The Secretary met that crisis head-on, issuing a statement in a press release and moving swiftly to remove the officials responsible for the substandard care at Manchester.

The Hon. Michael Missal   February 11, 2018

you include a copy of this submission and its supporting documentation in its entirety as an
appendix to your final report.

Sincerely,

Justin Shur
Eric Nitz
Emily Damrau

Encls.

<u>**Declaration of Andrew D. Herman**</u>

I. Andrew D. Herman, hereby declare as follows:

1. I am a member of Miller & Chevalier, Chartered, located in Washington, DC. I am submitting this declaration at the behest of counsel for Secretary of Veterans Affairs David Shulkin, in response to the Draft Report prepared by the Office of Inspector General (OIG) for Veterans Affairs ("Draft Report"). The statements and information in this declaration are based on my analysis of the Draft Report; my review of applicable regulations and published guidance from the United States Office of Government Ethics (OGE) and others; and my close to 20 years of experience as an attorney practicing in the area of government ethics.

2. As set forth in greater detail below, it is my opinion that, under applicable ethics regulations, Secretary Shulkin's acceptance of Wimbledon tickets was proper; the OIG does not establish that Secretary Shulkin received an improper gift. The Draft Report utilizes 5 C.F.R. § 2635.201 to find impropriety. That provision, however, is a subjective, non-binding standard that does not create liability under the OGE's Standards of Conduct. While the Draft Report also utilizes certain terms applicable to 5 C.F.R. § 2635.202, the general gift prohibition, it presents neither facts nor analysis establishing a violation of that regulation.

<u>**Background and Qualifications**</u>

3. I graduated from the University of California, Hastings College of the Law in 1996. In 1999, I joined the law firm of Brand, Lowell & Ryan, where I practiced until 2013, when I joined Miller & Chevalier, my current firm. During my career, I have represented members of the United States Senate and House and their staff before the Senate and House Ethics Committees. Overall, I have represented more than two dozen clients in congressional ethics matters. I currently represent several clients in ethics cases pending before the House Committee on Ethics. I have also represented individuals and entities in ethics-related civil litigation, including serving as counsel in two trials related to civil ethics charges brought by the United States Department of Justice. I counsel several non- profit organizations, labor unions and lobbying firms on campaign finance rules, lobbying disclosure and compliance with applicable ethics rules and regulations. I am frequently quoted in the media regarding newsworthy ethics issues.

<u>**Ethics Regulations Relating to Analysis in the Draft Report**</u>

4. The Draft Report evaluates Secretary Shulkin's acceptance of tickets to the Wimbledon Ladies' Final Match on July 15, 2017, from Victoria Gosling.

5. The Draft Report first cites to 5 C.F.R. § 2635.201, the OGE regulation titled "Overview and considerations for declining otherwise permissible gifts." In

promulgating the regulation, the OGE described § 2635.201 as "a non-binding standard that can assist employees in considering whether to decline an otherwise permissible gift." *See* Standards of Ethical Conduct for Employees of the Exec. Branch; Amendments to Standards on Acceptance of Gifts, 81 Fed. Reg. 81,641, 81,641 (Nov. 18, 2016) (to be codified at 5 C.F.R. pt. 2635). The OGE also noted that "an employee will not face disciplinary action in the event that someone later subjectively disagrees with the employee's analysis" regarding whether a gift is permissible. *Id.* at 81,642.

6.   Section 2635.201 asks employees to consider several factors in assessing whether to accept an otherwise permissible gift: "(i) The gift has a high market value; (ii) The timing of the gift creates the appearance that the donor is seeking to influence an official action; (iii) The gift was provided by a person who has interests that may be substantially affected by the performance or nonperformance of the employee's official duties; and (iv) Acceptance of the gift would provide the donor with significantly disproportionate access." 5 C.F.R. § 2635.201(b)(2).

7.   While the Draft Report does not cite to 5 C.F.R. § 2635.202, the OGE regulation establishing a "[g]eneral prohibition on solicitation or acceptance of gifts," it discusses concepts relating to that section—including gifts from a "prohibited source," gifts given because of an employee's "official position" and the "personal relationship" exception to the rule. As such, for the purposes of my analysis, I have assumed that the Draft Report utilized § 2635.202 in concluding that Secretary Shulkin accepted an improper gift.

8.   Sections 2635.202(a) & (b) establish that an employee may not solicit or receive a gift from a "prohibited source" or because of the "employee's official position."
    Section 2635.203(d) defines a "prohibited source" as any person who: "(1) Is seeking official action by the employee's agency; (2) Does business or seeks to do business with the employee's agency; (3) Conducts activities regulated by the employee's agency; (4) Has interests that may be substantially affected by the performance or nonperformance of the employee's official duties."

9.   Section 2635.203(e) states that a "gift is given because of the employee's official position if the gift is from a person other than an employee and would not have been given had the employee not held the status, authority, or duties associated with the employee's Federal position."

10.   Section 2635.204(b) addresses the "personal relationship" exception to the prohibition on certain gifts: "An employee may accept a gift given by an individual under circumstances which make it clear that the gift is motivated by a family relationship or personal friendship rather than the position of the employee. Relevant factors in making such a determination include the history and nature of

the relationship and whether the family member or friend personally pays for the gift."

11.   The Draft Report also discusses the market value of the tickets at issue. Section 2635.203(c) provides that the "market value of a gift of a ticket entitling the holder to food, refreshments, entertainment, or any other benefit is deemed to be the face value of the ticket."

2

Relevant Factual Background

12. Secretary Shulkin traveled to London as the leader of a delegation attending the Ministerial Summit on Veterans' Affairs, held from July 18-20, 2017. Draft Report at 2.

Secretary Shulkin was invited to attend the Summit by the United Kingdom Parliamentary Under Secretary of State and Minister for Defense Personnel and Veterans. *Id.* The Summit, which is held every 18-24 months, addresses "challenges facing the veteran communities of Australia, Canada, New Zealand, the United Kingdom, and the United. States." *Id.*

13. Secretary Shulkin accepted two tickets to the Wimbledon tennis Ladies' Final Match on July 15, 2017, from Victoria Gosling. The Draft Report describes Ms. Gosling as a "UK resident and the Head of Social Impact at Auden, a for-profit enterprise; a Military Director of Sage Foundation, the philanthropic affiliate of UK software company Sage Group plc; and a Military Councilor for the Lawn Tennis Association, which is the national governing body for tennis in Great Britain, including Wimbledon. Ms. Gosling also served as CEO of the 2016 Invictus Games held in Orlando, Florida." Draft Report at 9. However, when they spoke at Wimbledon, Ms. Gosling informed Secretary Shulkin that she "was not employed but was looking at a number of options." *Id.* at 12.

Under Applicable Ethics Regulations, Secretary Shulkin's Acceptance of Wimbledon Tickets Was Proper

14. In concluding that Secretary Shulkin accepted an improper gift, the Draft Report does not cite to 5 C.F.R. § 2635.202, the general prohibition on the solicitation or acceptance of certain gifts. I interpret this omission as a tacit admission by the OIG that, after an extensive investigation, it cannot conclude that Secretary Shulkin violated that prohibition. However, the Draft Report does rely on terminology derived from the regulation. *See* Draft Report at 15-16.

15. Section 2635.202 bars federal employees from soliciting or accepting a gift from a

"prohibited source," or one given because of the employee's "official position."

16. The Draft Report asserts that, "[b]y virtue of her business relationships (whether for profit or not), Ms. Gosling may also meet the definition of a 'prohibited source.'" Draft Report at 16. Beyond offering this equivocal statement—and failing to cite to the relevant gift prohibition—the Draft Report makes no attempt to assess whether Ms. Gosling's interests at the time she made the gift qualify her as "prohibited source," as defined by § 2635.203(d)(1) through (5).

17. The Draft Report provides no evidence that Ms. Gosling—whom Secretary Shulkin believed was unemployed at the time of their meeting (*see* Draft Report at 12)—was seeking official action from the VA, doing business with the VA, conducting activities regulated by the VA or had interests that might be substantially affected by Secretary Shulkin's official duties. A substantive "prohibited source" analysis s would require that the OIG assess Ms. Gosling's actual interests relating to Secretary Shulkin and the VA at

3

the time that she made the gift. In the absence of such an assessment by the OIG, there is no basis for the Draft Report to conclude that Ms. Gosling was a "prohibited source."

18. The Draft Report does assert that Ms. Gosling "requested Secretary Shulkin's assistance in gaining an invitation to the London Summit" that Secretary Shulkin was attending. Draft Report at 14. Although Secretary Shulkin informed the OIG that he did not assist Ms. Gosling in any way (*id.* at 14 n.26), the purported request is not material to the

"prohibited source" analysis. If it occurred, Ms. Gosling's request for assistance in attending the London Summit would not implicate any of § 2635.203(d)'s factors relating to official actions that could be undertaken by Secretary Shulkin or the VA.

19. In light of the facts presented in the Draft Report, it is my opinion that Ms. Gosling was not a prohibited source at the time that she made the gift to Secretary Shulkin.

20. The Draft Report also asserts, without citing to the term's regulatory definition, that Ms. Gosling provided the tickets because of Secretary Shulkin's "official position." Draft Report at 15. In reaching this conclusion, the Draft Report states, "[p]rior to Wimbledon, there was no evidence that Secretary Shulkin or his wife met with Ms. Gosling at an event other than the three gatherings he attended in his official capacity." *Id.* at 15-16.

21. Without further explanation and analysis, the OIG's conclusion is a *non-sequitur*. That Secretary Shulkin first met Ms. Gosling in his official capacity (years before he was Secretary) in no way establishes that he received the gift because of his

current position. *See* Example 1 to 5 C.F.R. § 2635.203(e) (where free tickets are offered to "all members of the Cabinet," a gift is given because of employee's official position). Both Secretary Shulkin and Ms. Gosling repeatedly disclaimed any official connection and the OIG presents no evidence that Ms. Gosling provided the tickets because of Secretary Shulkin's position, rather than because of their preexisting personal connection.

22. Because the Draft Report (1) does not find that Secretary Shulkin's receipt of the tickets violated § 2635.202's general prohibition on gifts, and (2) does not establish that Ms. Gosling was a prohibited source, there is no need to address whether the "personal relationship" exception is applicable pursuant to § 2635.204(b).

23. In concluding that "Ms. Gosling gave a gift of the Wimbledon tickets, which were very valuable on the secondary market, because of Secretary Shulkin's official position," the Draft Report cites to and relies on 5 C.F.R. § 2635.201. Draft Report at 15. This conclusion incorrectly applies the plain language of the regulation and the OGE's interpretation of the hortatory language.

24. Section 2635.201 imposes no prohibition on an employee's acceptance of a gift. Instead, it creates "a **non-binding standard** that can assist employees in considering whether to decline **an otherwise permissible gift**." *See* 81 Fed. Reg. 81,641, 81,641 (Nov. 18, 2016) (emphasis added).

4

25. While the OIG may subjectively believe that Secretary Shulkin should not have accepted the Wimbledon tickets, § 2635.201 does not provide authority for the OIG to impose any sanction. As OGE General Counsel David J. Apol wrote in a December 21, 2016 legal advisory to Designated Agency Ethics Officials, "[t]he new section makes clear that an employee who accepts a gift permitted under an applicable exception will not be deemed to have violated the Standards of Conduct." 81 Fed Reg. at 81,649 (to be codified at 5 C.F.R. § 2635.201(b)(3))."

26. Even if the OIG simply wishes to indicate its subjective disapproval of Secretary Shulkin's acceptance of the tickets under § 2635.201, the Draft Report fails to assess adequately the four elements listed in § 2635.201(b)(2) (i-iv) that "employees may consider when determining whether to decline an otherwise permissible gift." 81 Fed. Reg. at 81,642-81,643.

27. The Draft Report only directly addresses the "market value" of the tickets. *See* § 2635.201(b)(2)(i) (a relevant factor is whether tickets have "high market value"). This assessment is also the source for the OIG's recommendation that Secretary Shulkin reimburse the cost of the "tangible benefits" provided by Ms. Gosling. Draft Report at 25.

28. The OIG states that it "was not able to determine the availability and cost of 2017 Wimbledon tickets on commercial websites." Draft Report at 9 n.19. Instead, the OIG determined that the price for 2018 Wimbledon tickets on "commercial websites" was "£1,205.00 (approx. $1,760)." *Id.* This analysis does not comport with the OGE's regulation for determining the market value of a gift.

29. Section 2635.203(c) provides that the "market value of a gift of a ticket entitling the holder to food, refreshments, entertainment, or any other benefit is deemed to be the face value of the ticket." *See also* Legal Advisory to designated Agency Ethics Officials Presidential Inaugural Events, OGE Informal Advisory Letter LA-16-11, 2016 WL 7404631, at *1 (Dec. 20, 2016); Standards of Ethical Conduct for Employees of the Executive Branch, 57 Fed. Reg. 35,006-01 (Aug. 7, 1992) (considering and rejecting argument that tickets should be valued at an amount higher than face value). The 2017 Wimbledon website—which has remained accessible on the internet at this URL: https://www.wimbledon.com/en_GB/atoz/tickets_and_ticket_prices.html—lists the maximum value of the 2017 Centre Court tickets as £155 (approximately $215) and No.1 Court standing admission at £34 (approximately $46). Ms. Gosling told the OIG that she purchased the tickets at a "discount." Draft Report at 15 n.31. Accordingly, these prices listed by Wimbledon represent the maximum price at which OIG may value the tickets.

30. While the Draft Report ignores the other considerations in § 2635.201, their application does not support its conclusion either. The second factor asks whether the "timing of the gift creates an appearance that the donor is seeking to influence an official action." § 2635.201(b)(2)(ii). The Draft Report demonstrates that the timing of the gift was simply tied to the date of the tennis match, rather than any official action by Secretary Shulkin. Draft Report at 10.

5

31. Section 2635.201(b)(2)(iii) asks whether "the gift was provided by a person who has interests that may substantially affected be the performance or nonperformance of the employee's official duties." As I discussed in paragraphs 20 and 21, there is no indication in the Draft Report that Ms. Gosling provided the gift for any official reason.

32. Finally, the single meal shared by the group does not satisfy the "frequent" interactions contemplated by § 2635.201(b)(2)(iv)'s "significantly disproportionate access" consideration. *See* 81 Fed. Reg. at 81,643

(disproportionate access "concern can arise in connection with gifts such as frequent" events).

33. After examining the information contained in the Draft Report, it is my opinion that, under applicable ethics regulations, Secretary Shulkin's acceptance of Wimbledon tickets was proper. Because the Draft Report incorrectly applies both the plain language of the regulations and the OGE's interpretation of those regulations, it is also my opinion that the Draft Report does not establish that Secretary Shulkin received an improper gift.

I declare under the penalty of perjury that the foregoing is true and correct.

Executed on February 11, 2018   Andrew D. Herman

<u>**DECLARATION OF VICTORIA GOSLING, O.B.E.**</u>

I, Victoria Gosling, O.B.E., declare as follows:

1.   I am a citizen of the United Kingdom and an Officer of the Order of the British Empire. I currently reside in England.

2.   I retired from the Royal Air Force in April of 2017. As of July 2017, I held a number of part-time jobs. At no point since my retirement have I done business with the Department of Veterans Affairs (VA), nor have I sought to do business with the VA. Likewise, none of my employers have done business with the VA or sought to do business with the VA during that time.

3.   I have known VA Secretary David Shulkin and his wife, Merle Bari, since 2015, and I consider them my personal friends. I first met David and Merle in 2015 at an event at the British Embassy in the United States. I immediately recognized that there was a lot of synergy between Merle and myself. We both are avid fans of tennis and got along very well.

4.   I saw David and Merle again in 2016, when I was CEO of the Invictus Games. Orlando was hosting the Games that year, and David and Merle were attending. As at the British Embassy, Merle and I carried on like old friends. We discussed tennis and other personal matters. For the two of us, the conversation was purely social. We never discussed business. In fact, I don't know what 'business' we could even have discussed!

5.   In April 2017, I met up with David and Merle again. As always, it was wonderful seeing them. Merle and I of course discussed tennis. We also generally caught up with what was going on in each other's lives.

6.   I understand that, around this time, ███████████ a mutual acquaintance, reached out to David saying that I had asked her for an introduction to David. I never asked

████ to introduce me to David. I had, of course, known David for several years by that point. I do not know why ████ made that inquiry of David. Perhaps there was a misunderstanding.

7. When I saw Merle at those events in 2015, 2016, and 2017, my conversations with her were not superficial. To the contrary, we spent significant amounts of time chatting. Whilst David may have been attending these functions in his capacity as a government official, I never felt like my conversations with Merle were official government business or professional in any way. I felt like I was talking with a personal friend—because I was. I genuinely enjoyed spending time with Merle, and I think she likewise enjoyed spending time with me. To be honest, I think Merle was grateful that she had a friend to talk to at events like these. David would often be 'making the rounds' among the guests. Having the opportunity to talk tennis with me probably made these events more tolerable for Merle.

8. Given the nature of my interactions with Merle, it was somewhat embarrassing for me when I was recently interviewed by representatives from the VA Office of Inspector General and could not remember Merle's name. The investigators unexpectedly called me on my mobile phone whilst I was driving on a very busy highway. I felt like the investigators were twisting my words and trying to put words in my mouth. At the very end of the interview, the investigators—who had only referred to Merle as David's 'wife'—asked me what David's 'wife' was called. Given the nature of the interview, I felt put on the spot and I was already flustered and could not remember Merle's name. I do, in fact, know Merle's first name. I do consider her my friend.

9. I haven't visited the United States for a while, however, should I be planning a visit, then I would definitely make contact with Merle and David to see if we could meet up. I would hope that, whenever Merle and David travel to London, they would let me know. Our

relationship was such that I would have been upset if I'd found out that Merle was in the U.K. and had not reached out to connect. I was thus very excited when Merle mentioned to me that she and David would be visiting London. I told her that we all had to arrange a time to meet up—her, David, myself, and my husband.

10.   Sometime in June 2017, David emailed me to ask for recommended tourist sites in London and to inquire where he might be able to purchase tickets to Wimbledon. His timing was fortuitous. I was the Military Councillor to the Lawn Tennis Association, which is a voluntary position and entitles me to purchase a book of tickets which includes a pair of tickets to each day of Wimbledon at a discounted rate. I had purchased two tickets for my sister on July 15 which cost me a total of £155. Right before I read David's email, my sister had called to say that she was no longer able to attend the match.

11.   Because I had the extra pair of tickets, I offered them to David out of friendship. I knew how much Merle loves tennis, and I knew how much she would enjoy Wimbledon. I also invited Merle, David, and their son to join me and my husband for lunch prior to the match. I had so enjoyed spending time with them—particularly Merle—in the United States that I looked forward to seeing them in London. Their visit to Wimbledon was delightful. We of course talked a lot about tennis, and even discussed attending the U.S. Open when I visited the United States.

12.   David offered to pay me for the tickets—several times, in fact. Even before we attended the match, David had emailed to ask how much he owed me. He raised the subject again in person when we met in London. Each time, I politely declined. I invited David and Merle as my friends and guests. I wasn't going to accept their payment for the time we enjoyed together. Moreover, it is important to note that the LTA restrictions on purchasing a book of

discounted Centre Court tickets prevent me from 'selling on' tickets to a third party. I simply told them that Merle could repay me by taking me out to dinner the next time I visited the United States.

13.   Admittedly, I don't communicate with Merle and David as much as I would like. With three children and an active professional life, I don't have much time. (In fact, months will sometimes pass when I don't speak to my own sister.) The time difference and distance between London and the United States only makes things more difficult. But as I explained above, I would always make an effort to meet up with David and Merle when I travel to the United States, and I would be deeply hurt if they did not let me know when their travels brought them to the U.K. That we do not trade emails on a weekly or daily basis, that we do not regularly chat on the phone—none of that, for me at least, diminishes the value of our friendship.

14.   I gave the Wimbledon tickets to Merle and David because I considered them my friends. Merle and David are generally very supportive and helpful people. David has done so much for veterans in his country and mine. I felt that taking Merle and David to Wimbledon would be a nice way to thank them for their personal support of me over the years. I never suggested to David or Merle that the Wimbledon tickets were a 'thank you' for anything, though.

15.   I did not give the tickets to David because of his position or for anything David had done in his position. In fact, if David had rejoined the private sector and reached out to me as he had done, I would have done exactly the same thing—offered him and Merle the tickets, taken them to lunch, and enjoyed their company. I neither expected nor asked David to do anything for me in exchange for the tickets. Nor did David offer to do anything—or actually do anything—for me in exchange for the tickets, other than his several offers to pay for them. I also

did not buy the tickets specifically for Merle and David. It just so happened that my sister had to

cancel. If my sister had not cancelled, I would not have offered them the tickets.

     I declare under penalty of perjury under the laws of the United States of America that the
foregoing is true and correct.

Executed on: February _11_, 2018

In: _Westminster, England_

Victoria Gosling
Victoria Gosling, O.B.E.

Calendar for July 2017 Official Trip to Europe

July 2017

Sunday	Monday	Tuesday	Wednesday	Thursday	Friday	Saturday
9	10	11 Secretary treats patients at NY VA Transit to Copenhagen	12 Arrive in Copenhagen Attending to VA work	13 Danish conference Attending to VA work, U.S. Embassy dinner	14 Danish conference	15 Transit to London Attending to VA work
16 Attending to VA work	17 Attending to VA work	18 Attending to VA work, Reception for London conference	19 London conference	20 London conference	21 Transit to U.S.	22

Signifies time on official work or events

Appendix E

February 12, 2018, Response of the VA Secretary

79

THE SECRETARY OF VETERANS AFFAIRS

WASHINGTON

February 12, 2018
The Honorable Michael J. Missal
Inspector General
Department of Veterans Affairs
801 I Street, N.W.
Washington, D.C. 20001

Re:: *Administrative Investigation Draft Report*

Dear Inspector General Missal:

This letter is in reference to the report concerning your administrative investigation into my official travel to the conferences in both Copenhagen and London. Shockingly, it appears a draft version of the report has already been leaked from your office before I had an opportunity to respond. What is more troubling, though, is that the report does not appear accurate or objective, and it contains the thread of bias. A report of this nature is a direct assault on my spouse, my character, and my unblemished record of service to the Veterans Affairs Administration.

I am proud of my 32 year career as a physician and a medical administrator. Under the previous administration, I agreed to leave the private sector, displacing my family, to serve the Veterans Affairs Administration. My duty has been to serve our nation's veterans and provide them with the care and service they deserve. In light of historical integrity problems that have plagued the VA, I have also made it a core objective to root out corruption and negligence. I am proud that my service has granted me the ability to serve as Secretary under President Donald J. Trump.

I identify several problems with the accuracy of your report, as well as the way you have conducted this ongoing investigation. The current draft report, which I received on February 7th, ignores critical facts, improperly applies the relevant regulations, and draws conclusions based on subjective and arbitrary criteria. It appears to present a foregone conclusion regardless of the full facts of the matter.

First, I take serious issue with how you've depicted my wife, Merle. Merle has made many sacrifices throughout my career in government, including the routine purchase of train travel and cancellation of office hours in her private physician practice to join me in Washington. In the case of our European trip last Summer, my wife was officially invited to accompany me – as spouses of cabinet members often do – to the conferences in both Copenhagen and London. Your office has attempted to make political fodder of her being by my side, made possible by taking a commercial flight in a coach seat that was pre-approved by our ethics department. To be clear, it was the VA that suggested her travel be paid for by the VA, as has been the practice for other spouses in similar situations. To clarify once again, I had *nothing* to do with the process of obtaining approval for my wife's travel or otherwise planning the day-to-day travel arrangements. Those tasks were delegated to my staff, and I reasonably relied on them to comply with all applicable rules and regulations. It is outrageous that you would portray my wife and me as attempting to take advantage of the government.

Second, your report forms an inappropriate judgment regarding what my family chooses to do with our free time on a Saturday afternoon. My wife and I did what millions of people do every day. We went to a sporting event, on our personal time, with a friend. Our friend neither has business with nor seeks to do business with the VA. She purchased her tickets privately, and we offered to reimburse her on several occasions – a fact your office is aware of but chose to disregard in your report.

Third, the entire report seeks to question and undermine the validity of the trip and its importance to furthering the work of the Veterans Administration. As already explained but disregarded in your report, I met with the Danish Ministry of Health to discuss healthcare implementation and the Danish Minister of Defense regarding veterans' policies. The Five Eyes Ministerial Summit on Veterans' Affairs in London – which has regularly been attended by past VA Secretaries – was similarly valuable given the Summit's focus on mental health issues facing veterans. It is a part of my job to continually learn about and actively participate in the developing issues facing veterans. To suggest that such meetings have an indeterminate value reflects a fundamental misunderstanding of my duties and the mission of the VA as a whole.

I also want to express that I am deeply concerned over how your office has conducted this investigation over the past several months. Despite going through proper channels and seeking independent approvals, providing transparent accounting of my travel, and fully cooperating with your investigation, you have treated the staff of the Veterans Administration, my wife, and my friends with extreme contempt, bordering on badgering and harassment. Your staff's conduct related to this investigation reeks of an agenda. Your portrayal of this trip is overall and entirely inaccurate.

When someone shines a flashlight on a problem at the VA, I have publically invited floodlight scrutiny of the issue, so I fully understand the importance of your Office's mission. If you had properly considered my testimony and recognition of the facts of this case, however, I am confident that you would have concluded that I have conducted myself properly, ethically and in-line with how I have always served the Veterans Administration. *Substantial revisions are needed to ensure that the report accurately describes the events in question and conveys findings that are appropriately supported by the facts.* I look forward to working with you to correct this report. It is unfortunate that your initial report, which has already been leaked, is so fundamentally flawed.

It is important that moving forward we all remain focused on the continued improvements required for our country's veterans. Despite the unfair allegations of this report directed at me and having done nothing improper, it is essential that our veterans know that all of VA's resources are dedicated to this single purpose. I have submitted additional information detailing my concerns with this draft report and ask for your consideration of this new information that has not yet been properly considered. If after full and *fair* consideration of these additional items, it is still your recommendation that I reimburse the Treasury for the coach airfare and the costs associated with the tennis event to my wife's friend, I will comply.

Sincerely,

David J. Shulkin, M.D.

Appendix F

February 11, 2018, Response of the VA Deputy Secretary

VA Office of Inspector General   82

February 11, 2018

The Honorable Michael Missal
Inspector General
Office of the Inspector General
U.S. Department of Veterans Affairs

Subject: VA Response to Final Draft Report of Investigation on the "Administrative Investigation of VA Secretary and Delegation Travel to Europe".

Dear Mr. Missal:

Due to the unique nature of this report with allegations involving the Secretary of Veterans Affairs Secretary I have assumed, with his approval, the responsibilities of agency head for the purposes of responding to this report.

On February 5th I received a copy of the Department of Veterans Affairs Office of the Inspector General (OIG) draft report on the "Administrative Investigation of VA Secretary and Delegation Travel to Europe". I was informed a copy was also provided to the VA Secretary. On Thursday morning, February 8th, I received from the OIG another version of the final draft of this report of investigation. I again was told at that time that I had until COB Friday, the following day, to review the report and provide the Department's comments to those recommendations directed to me for action. I immediately had questions about those recommendations and whose responsibility it was to respond to the recommendations one and two which involved the VA Secretary. Subsequently at 10:31 AM on Thursday I received what I was again informed was a final amendment to the recommendations.

That same Thursday evening the VA General Counsel sent the Inspector General an email stating that the time frame OIG had established for the Department to review and respond to the draft report was inadequate to enable the Department to properly review the report and extensive supporting documentation and provide an informed decision on whether to agree or disagree with the recommendations. On Friday morning February 9th the Counselor to the Inspector General responded to the General Counsel saying that the IG was willing to "extend" the deadline for the Department's response from COB today until 6:00 PM Sunday, February 11th. Even with the new deadline the Department would have had less than two work days (three and a half total days) to review and consider its response. I believe this is entirely inappropriate and contrary to the established procedures of the OIG of granting 30 days in other cases, especially those of lesser significance.

It is important that the Department have adequate time to carefully understand and evaluate the OIG draft report and develop a response to agree or disagree with the report recommendations. OIG has been conducting its review of this matter for more than six months. The evidence files that OIG has provided that serve as the basis for the report are extensive. The report raises significant legal issues which the Office of General Counsel and the must have the opportunity to consider before the Department can concur in your recommendations. I can conceive of no legitimate rationale for not providing the Department a reasonable opportunity to perform its due diligence. I suggest that imposing this extraordinary short deadline calls into question whether the IG has conducted a complete and objective review of these matters.

As the Counselor to the IG stated in his email to the General Counsel, "a 30 day time period [for responding to OIG draft reports] is common". However the rationalization that in this case there are only five recommendations and no specific action by the Department is required in order to respond is an inaccurate characterization of the report and is unreasonable when considering the impact on the agency, the Secretary and others involved in the report. The report involves complex legal issues. The facts relating to initiation and authorization of the various travel arrangements are not clear. I am also concerned that the draft report reflects that there was significant consultation with the VA Designated Agency Ethics Official (DAEO) and that it appears that the Secretary acted in compliance with advice that the DAEO gave. Understanding the confusion or alleged misrepresentation of the facts as presented in the report upon which the DAEO opined is very important to the Department and is not apparent on the face of the report.

Professionalism, due diligence and due process expect and require me to conduct a thorough review of the report and the large volume of supporting documentation. I am not aware of any occasion when the IG has so restricted the Department's opportunity to review a report. The inexplicable denial of a reasonable time to respond and urgency to publish the report compels a concern whether there is some unarticulated motivation by the IG to act outside the acceptable and experienced protocols for response times.

Although I have not had an opportunity to review the documentation that accompanies it, I am inordinately concerned that the report as written appears to take every opportunity to cast the VA, the Secretary and others identified in the report in the least favorable light through negative commentary or inferences.

Recommendation 1

The Secretary does not agree with the OIG conclusions of fact and law relating to this recommendation as presented in the OIG report, however he will consult with the Office of General Counsel and if it is determined that he should reimburse the Department for any part of Dr. Bari's travel costs he will do so.

Recommendation 2

The Secretary does not agree with the OIG conclusions of fact and law relating to this recommendation, however, he will consult with the Office of General Counsel and if it is determined that he should reimburse Ms. Gosling for any aspect of his attendance at Wimbledon, he will do so. (If Ms. Gosling declines to accept reimbursement, the Secretary will reimburse such amount to the U.S. Treasury.)

Recommendations 3

The Department has been inappropriately compelled and had an inadequate opportunity to review and respond to the Inspector General's report and the evidence that accompanied it. When the Department has completed its review the Deputy Secretary will in inform OIG as to whether it will accept this recommendation.

Recommendations 4

The Department has been inappropriately compelled and had an inadequate opportunity to review and respond to the Inspector General's report and the evidence that accompanied it. When the Department has completed its review the Deputy Secretary will in inform OIG as to whether it will accept this recommendation.

Recommendations 5

The Department has been inappropriately compelled and had an inadequate opportunity to review and respond to the Inspector General's report and the evidence that accompanied it. When the Department has completed its review the Deputy Secretary will in inform OIG as to whether it will accept this recommendation.

Thomas G. Bowman

Appendix G

OIG Contact and Staff Acknowledgments

OIG Contact   For more information about this report, please contact the Office of Inspector General at (202) 461-4720

Acknowledgments
<u>Office of Investigations</u>
Linda Fournier, Director
Alexander Carlisle, Deputy Director
Charles Millard, Senior Administrative Investigator

Domingo Alvarez, Administrative Investigator
Jason James, Administrative Investigator
Jacob Lay, Administrative Investigator
Leanne Shelly Watkins, Administrative Investigator
Michael Smith, Administrative Investigator William Tully, Administrative Investigator

<u>Office of the Counselor to the Inspector General</u>
Christopher Wilber, Counselor to the Inspector General
Clifford Stoddard, Attorney Advisor
R. James Mitchell, Attorney Advisor

<u>Office of eDiscovery</u>
Debbie Crawford, Program Manager
Scott Eastman, Supervisory Management and Program Analyst
Ashley Shingler, Management Analyst

<u>Office of Inspector General</u>
Martha Plotkin, Special Assistant to the Inspector General

Report Distribution

VA Distribution

Secretary and Deputy Secretary
Veterans Health Administration
Veterans Benefits Administration
National Cemetery Administration
Assistant Secretaries
Office of General Counsel

Non-VA Distribution

House Committee on Veterans' Affairs
House Appropriations Subcommittee on Military Construction, Veterans Affairs, and
        Related Agencies
House Committee on Oversight and Government Reform
Senate Committee on Veterans' Affairs
Senate Appropriations Subcommittee on Military Construction, Veterans Affairs, and
        Related Agencies
Senate Committee on Homeland Security and Governmental Affairs
National Veterans Service Organizations
Government Accountability Office
Office of Management and Budget

Report Suspected Wrongdoing in VA Programs and Operations: 1-800-488-8244 www.va.gov/oig/hotline

[1] Quote by David Shulkin during exclusive USA Today interview, February 14, 2018.

[2] "VA Watchdog to Say Chief Wrongly Accepted Wimbledon Tickets, Airfare, but His Lawyers Blast Findings" by Donovan Slack, February 12, 2018, *USA Today*

[3] "VA Secretary Shulkin Worsens Scandal with Dubious Explanation" by Rachel Maddow, February 15, 2018, *The Rachel Maddow Show*, MSNBC

[4] https://www.merriam-webster.com/dictionary/lying

Chapter Three

Shulkin's Slant

"*Hypocrisy is the audacity to preach integrity from a den of corruption.*"

Wes Fesler

David Shulkin

After Secretary Shulkin found out the Office of Inspector General was investigating him and his wife's European vacation, he hired a high-powered Public Relations firm to try and spin the story to the public and veterans in the best light possible.

Furthermore, Shulkin retained a legal counsel to represent him. MoloLamken, is a law firm which specializes in complex litigation. Of the various areas the firm specializes, one is white collar criminal defense. Of the at least three lawyers Shulkin retained, one of them specializes in crisis management.

The firm representing Shulkin, prepared and sent a 16-page retort to the Office of Inspector General's anticipated formal report. Those 16 pages appeared above within the 97 pages of the Office of Inspector General's report.

The 16-pages of responses to the Office of Inspector General, rebuts the narrative that presents evidence of Shulkin's wrongdoing. The Office of Inspector General explained that their reports "must be accurate", "must be fair" and "must be objective." Shulkin's attorney stated, "*This report is none of those things.*"

The 16-page rebuttal included the following directed at the Office of Inspector General's report: "*It presents yet another example of your willingness to cherry-pick facts that support your sensationalist narrative rather than objectively report what happened.*"

Another copy and paste from Shulkin's law firm is: "*It* [the report] *ignores critical facts, presenting a one-sided version of events that casts aside evidence contradicting your chosen narrative. It improperly applies the relevant regulations, at times mischaracterizing them. And it imposes subjective and arbitrary criteria for evaluating the propriety of the Secretary's actions."*

"… simply underscores that your office did not approach this investigation in an objective and unbiased manner.

Shulkin's law firm had the following statements in their 16-page refutation. *"We left the Secretary's interview on December 14 with grave concerns about the objectivity and the fairness with which your office was pursuing this investigation. As we explained in our December 21 [2017] letter, the conduct of the investigators who interviewed the Secretary left us worried that those investigators were intent on portraying the Secretary unfavorably and were not impartially obtaining and evaluating the facts. Your Counselor, Mr. Wilber, responded that "it is the policy of OIG to review the facts and evidence collected in any matter . . . objectively and fairly." He assured us that your office "will do so here." That promise appears to have gone unfulfilled."*

"And your investigators have relied on interrogation techniques that have long since been recognized as unfair, unreliable, and abusive. Your report, moreover, confuses and misapplies legal standards in an effort to manufacture violations where none exist."

Shulkin initially put out a defiant statement saying he had been falsely accused. However, that statement was quickly taken down from the VA's web site, (www.VA.gov) and replaced with one in which he accepted responsibility for the multi-country travel boondoggle.

It begs the question. The Office of Inspector General is an Office <u>within</u> the Department of Veterans Affairs. If the Office of Inspector General is such a poorly run Office, then why during David Shulkin's approximately three years of leadership with the VA as the Under Secretary of Health and then in his current position as the Secretary of the VA, has he not complained about them? Why apparently is the first time Shulkin complains about the Office of Inspector General, the same time when they made public an incriminatory report about him?

The following is a tweet regarding Shulkin's above comments.

Whistleblower's Wife @VA_WB_Wife

@SecShulkin; #Whistleblowers know exactly how you feel. They experience leadership retaliation, being spied on, investigations tarnished reputations, removal of duties, silencing & the fear of being fired DAILY. It's part of the game, YOUR GAME! Not liking the rules now are you.

9:19 AM - 18 Feb 2018

Shulkin's firm had the following quote in their rebuttal. *"Your analysis is highly flawed, both factually and legally."* If Shulkin believes that the Director of the Office of Inspector General has generated a report that is *"highly flawed"*, then as Secretary of the VA, it is his responsibility to resolve this problematic Office. When whistleblowers report fraud, waste, abuse and substandard care, their disclosures are directed to the Office of Inspector General. This is disconcerting to me, a VA whistleblower, if it is true what Shulkin's law firm has stated in writing, that the Office of Inspector General is abysmal at investigating complaints.

The Office of Inspector General's report stated, **"Secretary Shulkin asked in April 2017 if VA could pay for his wife's travel expenses . . . ."**

In the 97-page Office of Inspector General's report, it states in September 2017, Shulkin tried to reimburse the person who provided him the free Wimbledon tennis tickets. It states, *"… you suggest that the Secretary only offered to pay for the tickets after The Washington Post inquired about them."*

Question: The tennis tournament was in <u>July</u>. Why in <u>September</u> did Shulkin try to reimburse the price of the free tickets he received for himself, his wife and his son?

David Shulkin explained that he did nothing wrong

As outlined already in Chapter 2, the following is an excerpt from Secretary Shulkin's interview with *The Washington Post.*

<u>Secretary Shulkin</u>: *"Well, this is your chance. Ask me any question you want."*

<u>Reporter</u>: *"Well, all right. The Wimbledon tickets."*

<u>Secretary Shulkin</u>: *"Yes?"*

<u>Reporter</u>: *"Did you buy those?"*

<u>Secretary Shulkin</u>: *"Yes"*

<u>Reporter</u>: *"Okay. So they weren't given to you as a gift by folks at the Invictus Games or anything like that?"*

<u>Secretary Shulkin</u>: *"No"*

In Shulkin's law firm's denial, they wrote the following quote regarding *The Washington Post's* interview of the Secretary. *"Nothing about the Secretary's statements was misleading."*

<u>Question</u>: Do you think the Secretary's statements were misleading?

"Secretary Shulkin directed [Mr. Gough] to coordinate with his wife to schedule the tourist activities that they wanted to do on non-official time."

Secretary Shulkin's assistant was *"... providing personal travel concierge services to Secretary Shulkin and his wife."*

Obviously, the above statements are very incriminating of the Secretary. Shulkin responded that certain members of his staff were plotting against him. Shulkin, worked closely with his public relations firm and legal counsel, and described this plotting and anonymous letter to the Director of the Office of Inspector General as **"subversive"** behavior.

<u>Question</u>: Do you think those VA employees; i.e.: the whistleblowers who sent the anonymous letter to the Office of Inspector General are wrong for disclosing Secretary Shulkin's European vacation which was paid for by federal taxpayers?

Shulkin was vague on who might be behind the plot against him but said there *"have been different people with agendas different than the one that I have and that has to stop."*

Following Vivieca Wright Simpson's abrupt retirement from her chief of staff position after the travel scandal broke in the news, the White House quickly (by the end of the same day) filled the position with Peter O'Rourke. Mr. O'Rourke, was Executive Director of the new VA Office of Accountability and Whistleblower Protection. Shulkin said, O'Rourke has the main responsibility for weeding out the plotters; i.e.: employees who made the anonymous whistleblower complaint to the Office of Inspector General.

Shulkin said O'Rourke had already begun meeting with those suspected of disloyalty (whistleblowers who sent the anonymous letter) *"individually and as a group to determine, now that there is a clear direction where we are going, where people are going to stand."*

<u>Question</u>: Do you think subversive behavior is another name for describing whistleblowers who sent the anonymous letter?

<u>Question</u>: Do you think purging whistleblowers is another name for retaliation?

Source: Becky Hand with permission

On February 16, 2018, two days after the Office of Inspector General made public the report of Shulkin's European travel scandal, VA chief of staff, Vivieca Wright Simpson retired. Per the Office of Inspector General's report, Ms. Simpson altered/misrepresented a federal document to increase the chance that Shulkin's wife's expenses would be paid for by federal taxpayers.

<u>Question</u>: Do you think Ms. Simpson should have been allowed to retire without being held accountable?

<u>Question</u>: Do you think there should be a criminal investigation about falsifying a federal document?

Rep. Mike Coffman @RepMikeCoffman

Question: For people who read Dr. Klein's book, *Scandals: Unmasking the Underbelly of the VA*, you are aware the United States Office of Special Counsel made a determination that Dr. Klein is a whistleblower and the VA retaliated against him. Subsequently, one administrator was transferred to another VA facility and another administrator was forced to retire one year earlier than he was planning. Do you think VA administrators who have been caught violating the law, should be transferred to another facility or allowed to retire without punitive actions against them?

Question: Do you think failure to initiate an investigation is a tacit endorsement of criminal behavior?

Shulkin Tried to Bring Wife to Invictus Games to Meet Prince Harry

By Brett Samuels, March 15, 2018, *The Hill*

Per the above article, Secretary Shulkin was scheduled to take an official business trip in September 2017 to Canada to attend the Invictus Games. Reportedly, Dr. Shulkin argued with White House staff that he wanted his wife to be able to attend the trip with him, because he was keen for her to meet Prince Harry. Shulkin was apparently miffed after the White House would not allow Shulkin's wife to reserve a seat on the airplane that would fly the Secretary and others to Canada.

However, after the European travel scandal story broke in the news media, Secretary Shulkin announced the official business trip he and his wife were planning to take to the Vatican, he cancelled.

Question: If the Shulkin European travel scandal had not been made public, do you think Shulkin and his wife would have made the trip to the Vatican on the taxpayers' dime?

Chapter Four

Ethical Responses

"Ethics is knowing the difference between what you have a right to do and what is right to do."

Potter Stewart: Associate Justice United States Supreme Court, 1958 to 1981

Walter Shaub, Esq.

Walter Shaub is an attorney and the former Director of the United States Office of Government Ethics. Mr. Shaub served in that capacity from January 9, 2013 to July 19, 2017. The ethical considerations of this European vacation spree, is well within the wheelhouse of Shaub to respond.

And respond Mr. Shaub did. Immediately after the story about Secretary Shulkin's European travel extravaganza broke in the news media, Shaub responded frequently and aggressively. Shaub did not mince words as he provided his insightful and expert opinions about the evolving federal scandal. Below are some of the tweets which appeared on Mr. Shaub's Twitter account.

Walter Shaub @waltshaub

Shulkin did not ask ethics officials before going to Wimbledon but he sought an

"expedited" ethics review after he learned of an impending Washington Post story, and

specifically told the ethics official that the donor was a "friend."

8:26 PM - 14 Feb 2018

Walter Shaub @waltshaub

@SecShulkin your conduct, as carefully presented in the OIG report, is appalling. You have dishonored your high office and you need to resign. The nation's veterans deserve better.
1:59 PM - 15 Feb 2018

Walter Shaub @waltshaub

Where is the rest of the Veterans Affairs committee? @RepMikeCoffman has it right. @SecShulkin must resign. Shulkin's conduct has been disgraceful and his explanation is preposterous. As Rep. Coffman said, it's not the optics that are not good, it's the facts that are not good.
Rep. Mike Coffman @RepMikeCoffman
It's exactly corruption and abuses like this that doesn't help our veterans. @SecShulkin must RESIGN now. @realDonaldTrump ran on accountability, it starts here. VA chief Shulkin, staff misled ethics officials about Eurotrip, report - The Washington Post https://www.washingtonpost.com/politics/veter
5:38 PM - 15 Feb 2018

Walter Shaub @waltshaub

Cowardly VA @SecShulkin blames his staff for his misconduct because, you know, the buck stops there. His Chief of Staff should have been fired for forging a federal record, not allowed to retire. And Shulkin himself MISLED ETHICS OFFICIALS. #ShulkinResign
9:37 AM - 16 Feb 2018

Walter Shaub @waltshaub

There is no overstating how thoroughly @SecShulkin has demonstrated his unfitness for federal service. While asking Congress for more firing authority, Shulkin has been committing acts that would get any VA employee fired. He must go. #ShulkinResign
7:25 AM - 18 Feb 2018

Walter Shaub @waltshaub

In my book, misleading agency ethics officials is a red line. Misusing a subordinate as a "personal travel concierge" ain't grand either. Neither is a boondoggle to Europe with your wife on the taxpayers' dime. Improper gifts, not so much either. Misleading the public? Nope.
1:21 PM - 20 Feb 2018

Walter Shaub @waltshaub

One week after a scathing IG investigative report reveals gross malfeasance by @SecShulkin, he announces a "purge" of those guilty of "subversion." This is shocking. **Back on Earth, we have a name for this sort of thing. We call it whistleblower retaliation.**
4:04 AM - 21 Feb 2018

Walter Shaub @waltshaub

A cabinet-level official leading a 370,000-employee agency publicly announces he'll "purge" those cooperating with an Inspector General who released a scathing investigative report about him, and it's not on the front page of every paper in the country. Are we lost as a nation?

> I also want to express that I am deeply concerned over how your office has conducted this investigation over the past several months. Despite going through proper channels and seeking independent approvals, providing transparent accounting of my travel, and fully cooperating with your investigation, you have treated the staff of the Veterans Administration, my wife, and my friends with extreme contempt, bordering on badgering and harassment. Your staff's conduct related to this investigation reeks of an agenda. Your portrayal of this trip is overall and entirely inaccurate.

6:58 AM - 21 Feb 2018

Walter Shaub @waltshaub

This is weak tea, Senators. You have got to do more here. Shulkin deceived an ethics official. In a government that lets cabinet officials deceive ethics officials, there is no ethics program.
7:28 PM - 22 Feb 2018

Walter Shaub @waltshaub

As promised, here is the case for terminating @SecShulkin. If a cabinet member can deceive an ethics official with impunity, it spells the end of the ethics program. I hope Members of Congress will read this piece and take appropriate action.

"In any Other Presidency, Our 'insufficiently accurate' Secretary of Veterans Affairs Would be Gone" by Walter Shaub, *Los Angeles Times*, Op-Ed, February 28, 2018
5:03 AM - 28 Feb 2018

But wait, there's more. Read below how a military veteran and current member of Congress reacted to the taxpayer-funded wasteful multi-country vacation enjoyed by the Secretary and his wife.

Mike Coffman
United States Congressman

Mr. Mike Coffman is a retired member of the U.S. Army and U.S. Marine Corps and served in the Gulf War and the Iraq War. And he has been in the United States House of Representatives since 2009.

On February 28, 2018, Congressman Coffman said in a letter to President Trump; the Secretary, *"clearly lacks the moral authority to lead."*

Furthermore, Congressman Coffman stated in the letter, *"When the leader of a department is seen as willing to violate or stretch the rules to personal advantage, the example set is unacceptable,"*

Coffman also wrote, *"Inevitably, employees throughout the VA will consider the example set by Secretary Shulkin as a 'green light' to avoid accountability."*

The two-page letter from Congressman Coffman to President Trump appears below.

MIKE COFFMAN
6TH DISTRICT, COLORADO

ARMED SERVICES COMMITTEE
MILITARY PERSONNEL
SUBCOMMITTEE CHAIRMAN

VETERANS' AFFAIRS COMMITTEE

2443 RAYBURN HOUSE OFFICE BUILDING
WASHINGTON, DC 20515
(202) 225-7882
(202) 226-4623 FAX

DISTRICT OFFICE:
3300 SOUTH PARKER ROAD
CHERRY CREEK PLACE IV, SUITE 305
AURORA, CO 80014
(720) 748-7514
(720) 748-7680 FAX

COFFMAN.HOUSE.GOV

Congress of the United States

House of Representatives

Washington, DC 20515–0606

February 28, 2018

The White House
Office of the President
1600 Pennsylvania Avenue, NW
Washington, DC 20500

Dear Mr. President:

I recently read the Department of Veterans Affairs (VA) Office of Inspector General (OIG) report: *"Administrative Investigation, VA Secretary and Delegation Travel to Europe."* This report concludes that VA Secretary, Dr. David J. Shulkin, intentionally misled government ethics officials and then lied to investigators to cover up the abuse of taxpayer's funds and government resources. Therefore, I write to ask you to relieve Secretary Shulkin of his current duties. I also request that you nominate as his replacement a true outsider to the VA's bureaucracy.

I am particularly concerned that, according to the OIG's report, the Secretary inappropriately accepted complimentary tickets to a Wimbledon tennis match from a Ms. Victoria Gosling. Then the Secretary knowingly mischaracterized Ms. Gosling as a friend of his wife (Dr. Bari) to ethics officials. The report indicates that he did so specifically to mislead the investigators into believing that these tickets qualified for the "personal friendship" exception to the rule prohibiting the acceptance of gifts. The OIG, however, found no evidence to document the existence of such friendship. In fact, upon sharing the additional information with the investigating ethics official, the OIG report states that Ms. Kennedy, the lead investigator on the examination, "concluded the 'totality of the documents totally indicate that they're not friends, as represented in Secretary Shulkin's response...'"

Then, when Dr. Shulkin was offered the opportunity to produce any documents to support his characterization of the relationship with Ms. Gosling as a personal friendship, the OIG report states that the Secretary "produced no evidence that his wife and Ms. Gosling communicated with one another outside of official events." This failed attempt to mischaracterize a relationship to gain an exception from ethics rules shows the Secretary's lack of respect for the guiding principles that ensure an ethical VA, cabinet, and government. In all, this VA OIG report clearly indicates that Dr. Shulkin violated the trust that you, the American people, and most importantly our veterans place in the individual responsible for Veterans Affairs.

Additionally, it appears that the Secretary did not follow his own guidance regarding official VA travel. On June 29, 2017, just two weeks before the Secretary's trip to Europe, Dr. Shulkin sent a memo to all VA employees demanding that all VA travel be "essential," as a cost-saving mechanism. According to the OIG report, the Secretary's eleven-day trip consisted of three and a half days of meetings, including an evening reception. Further, the report states that the schedule in Europe "included significant personal time for sightseeing and other unofficial activities." Based on the OIG's evidence and report, it is clear that Dr. Shulkin and his wife prioritized sightseeing at the expense of our nation's taxpayers. Similarly concerning, is the Secretary's failure to follow his own June 29th memo requiring that travel requests should "clearly document and retain the rationale for their decisions in the event travel requests are subsequently called into question." As a result, the OIG could not "determine whether the value of the trip to the VA, including the value provided by each participant in the trip, was consistent with the Secretary's memorandum." The OIG also determined that "inadequate documentation makes it impossible for the OIG to determine precisely which costs, if any, should have been borne by the traveler rather than the government." Although the OIG was able to calculate that the trip "cost the VA at least $122,334.00," we may never know the true cost of the Secretary's personal tourism to the taxpayers. This is unacceptable.

Finally, the OIG report concludes that the Secretary directed the misuse of VA resources. Specifically, that, "Secretary Shulkin directed VA Program Specialist Gough to work with Dr. Bari to plan personal activities for the Secretary and Dr. Bari during the trip." The report continues, "Mr. Gough was serving as a *de facto* personal travel concierge to the Secretary and his wife by providing detailed tourist planning and travel research services on official time at Secretary Shulkin's direction." Even more troubling, the OIG report indicates Secretary Shulkin failed to recognize the inappropriate nature of his request to Mr. Gough. Secretary Shulkin's use of Mr. Gough's official time in this manner is entirely inappropriate. I agree with the OIG's findings, "This was time that should have been spent conducting official VA business and not providing personal travel concierge services to Secretary Shulkin and his wife."

Based upon the facts provided in this OIG report, I believe that Secretary Shulkin clearly lacks the moral authority to lead the VA and the integrity expected of a member of your cabinet. When the leader of a department is seen as willing to violate or stretch the rules to personal advantage, the example set is unacceptable. Inevitably, employees throughout the VA will consider the example set by Secretary Shulkin as a "green light" to avoid accountability, to take opportunities for personal enrichment, or other violations of laws, regulations, and their duties.

Mr. President, you promised the American people that you would end the culture of corruption and bureaucratic incompetence that for far too long has defined the leadership of the VA. Unfortunately, Secretary Shulkin, by his conduct, lacks the moral authority to achieve your goals of a transparent, accountable VA that is dedicated to meeting our nation's obligations to the men and women who wore the uniform and made tremendous sacrifices in defense of our freedoms.

Thank you and I look forward to your response.

Sincerely,

Mike Coffman
Member of Congress

David Shulkin
Source: Aaron Bernstein, Getty Images

"there was never anything intentional."
Quote by Secretary Shulkin regarding the European travel scandal.
During exclusive *USA Today* interview, February 14, 2018

<u>Whistleblowers to Secretary Shulkin</u>: Dr. Shulkin, what was intentional about our actions? As whistleblowers, we made disclosures of fraud, waste, abuse and substandard care to try and save taxpayers' money and more importantly, improve veterans' care. But we got retaliated against. And some of us you fired. VA leadership, which you're responsible, mislead an ethics official for your personal gain. The VA has a culture of corruption. Where is the accountability Secretary Shulkin? We are patiently waiting…

That seems pretty bad, right? Then, Shulkin somehow made it even worse.

After the Office of Inspector General's report was released, Secretary Shulkin tried to justify why his chief of staff doctored a federal document to try and convince an ethics official to allow Shulkin's wife to have her trip paid for with taxpayers' money.

On February 15, 2018, the day after the Office of Inspector General's report was released to the public, Secretary Shulkin appeared before Congress at a House Veterans Committee meeting. During that meeting, Shulkin was asked about the Office of Inspector General's report. Shulkin tried to hoodwink Congress that his chief of staff had her email account hacked. And that it was not his chief of staff who modified the federal document but rather an email hacker.

A subsequent investigation that included the FBI, Department of Justice and led by the Office of Inspector General, found <u>no proof</u> the chief of staff's email had been hacked.

VA OIG Findings Create A Serious Credibility Problem for Shulkin In Hacking Claims[1]

By Luke Rosiak, Investigative Reporter, February 28, 2018, *The Daily Caller*

In this article, is the following quote by Congressman Mike Coffman. **"I believe that Secretary Shulkin clearly lacks the moral authority to lead the VA and the integrity expected of a member of your cabinet,"**.

And members of Congress were not the only ones perturbed by the actions of Secretary Shulkin. While Shulkin and his wife were on a taxpayers-funded trip to multiple foreign countries, a tourist who witnessed them apparently thought poorly of their royal treatment.

Susan Flickinger, is a U.S. citizen from the Madison, Wisconsin area. Ms. Flickinger was visiting an amusement park in Copenhagen, Denmark. While she was waiting in a long line, Shulkin and his entourage were whizzed to the front of the line without having to wait like the others.

Ms. Flickinger stated that one of Shulkin's security guards was carrying a "*large number of shopping bags.*" Per the news media report,[2] the VA did not respond to a request to answer questions about the trip.

<u>Question</u>: Do you think Secretary David Shulkin went swimming in ethically murky waters?

---

[1] http://dailycaller.com/2018/02/28/ig-shulkin-hacking-claims

[2] "Traveling in Style: Trump's White House Wrestles with Cabinet Costs" by Drew Harwell, Lisa Rein and Jack Gillum, October 8, 2017, *The Washington Post*

Chapter Five

Purge the Whistleblowers

Purge (Verb) *"To remove people from an area, country, organization, etc., often in a violent and sudden way."*[1]

Retaliate (Verb) *"To act in revenge."*[2]

Shulkin worked with his hired Public Relations company and multiple lawyers with his high-profile law firm he retained, to develop a strategy to overcome the bad publicity he created regarding the European travel scandal.

Shulkin says he has White House backing to purge VA

The embattled Cabinet head said he's investigating what he called 'subversion.'

By ARTHUR ALLEN | 02/20/2018 09:47 PM EST

"Shulkin Claims Mandate from White House to Purge Plotters at VA"

By Richard Sisk, February 21, 2018, *Military.com*

Shulkin <u>claimed</u> authorization from the White House to "purge" VA employees

Obviously, this European travel scandal distracted Secretary Shulkin, and others, from their primary focus of taking care of veterans. It appeared as if Shulkin is more interested in purging people who disclosed his European travel, instead of focused enthusiasm to improve the quality of care for veterans. Clearly, there are important veterans' issues to resolve. Nonetheless, the Secretary is fixated on the latest witch hunt to purge dissenters.

And speaking of whistleblowers, below are some totally irrational quotes from VA leadership.

"The leadership of VA protects whistleblowers and creates workplace environments that enable full participation of employees. We have zero tolerance for intimidation or retaliation – not just against whistleblowers, but against any employee who raises a hand to identify a problem, make a suggestion, or report what may be a violation in law, policy, or our core values."
Janet Murphy, Under Secretary for Health for Operations and Management
In a letter from Janet Murphy to Senator Robert Casey April 12, 2016

So, let me think out loud about Ms. Murphy's quote. The anonymous employees who sent the 10-page report to the Office of Inspector General that detailed wrongdoing by VA leadership is akin to raising *"a hand to identify a problem or report what may be a violation in law, policy, or our core values."* The same whistleblowers who raised their hand, are now in jeopardy of being purged for doing what Ms. Murphy encouraged to be done; i.e.: report a problem. This is exactly like my case, as I described in *Scandals: Unmasking the Underbelly of the VA.* I was encouraged by the Office of Inspector General to report wrongdoing. After making disclosures of fraud, waste, abuse and substandard care, I was terminated.

And this is a good time to reiterate Secretary Shulkin's own words in the following quote.

"And we will be investigating any issues related to retaliation. And the message is clear that we will not tolerate whistleblower retaliation in the Department of Veteran Affairs. And we will take actions if we do determine that retaliation has been imposed upon an employee who has come forth with an issue."
David Shulkin's Press Conference in the James S. Brady Briefing Room
April 26, 2017

Question: Do you think ~~firing~~ purging VA employees who are ~~whistleblowers~~ subversive, is appropriate/legal?

Dr. Carolyn Clancy is the current acting Undersecretary for Health at the VA. Dr. Clancy had the following quote in 2015.

Dr. Carolyn Clancy, chief medical officer for the Veterans Health Administration, the agency's health care arm, said the department's responsibility to protect whistleblowers *"is an integral part of our obligation to provide safe, high-quality health care. Retaliation against whistleblowers who have demonstrated the moral courage to share their concerns is unacceptable and cannot be tolerated."*
Carolyn Clancy, chief medical officer VA
"Whistleblowers: VA Inspector General a 'Joke'"
By Associated Press, September 22, 2015

Dr. Clancy's statement, appears to completely contradict Shulkin's scheme to purge the VA employees who are whistleblowers.

Furthermore, yet another quote that supports Shulkin should not take actions such as purging against those who reported violation of the law.

"If evidence emerges that employees, to include whistleblowers, have been treated unfairly for identifying important problems, immediate disciplinary actions will be taken against those who retaliate against them."
VA spokesperson
"Rally Held in Poplar Bluff, MO for VA Whistleblowers"
By Erin Elizabeth, May 16, 2017
https://www.healthnutnews.com/rally-held-poplar-bluff-mo-va-whistleblowers

Question: If the VA spokesperson above is correct, should Shulkin have immediate disciplinary actions taken against him if he would purge whistleblowers?

And finally, this quote from Curt Cashour, VA press secretary.

"VA does not tolerate retaliation."
Curt Cashour, VA press secretary
"Victims Say VA Whistleblower Retaliation is Growing Under Trump, Despite Rhetoric"
By Joe Davidson, October 30, 2017, *The Washington Post*

---

[1] https://www.merriam-webster.com/dictionary/purge

[2] https://www.merriam-webster.com/dictionary/retaliate

Chapter Six

Karma

"Karma (Noun) *The force created by a person's actions that some people believe causes good or bad things to happen to that person."*[1]

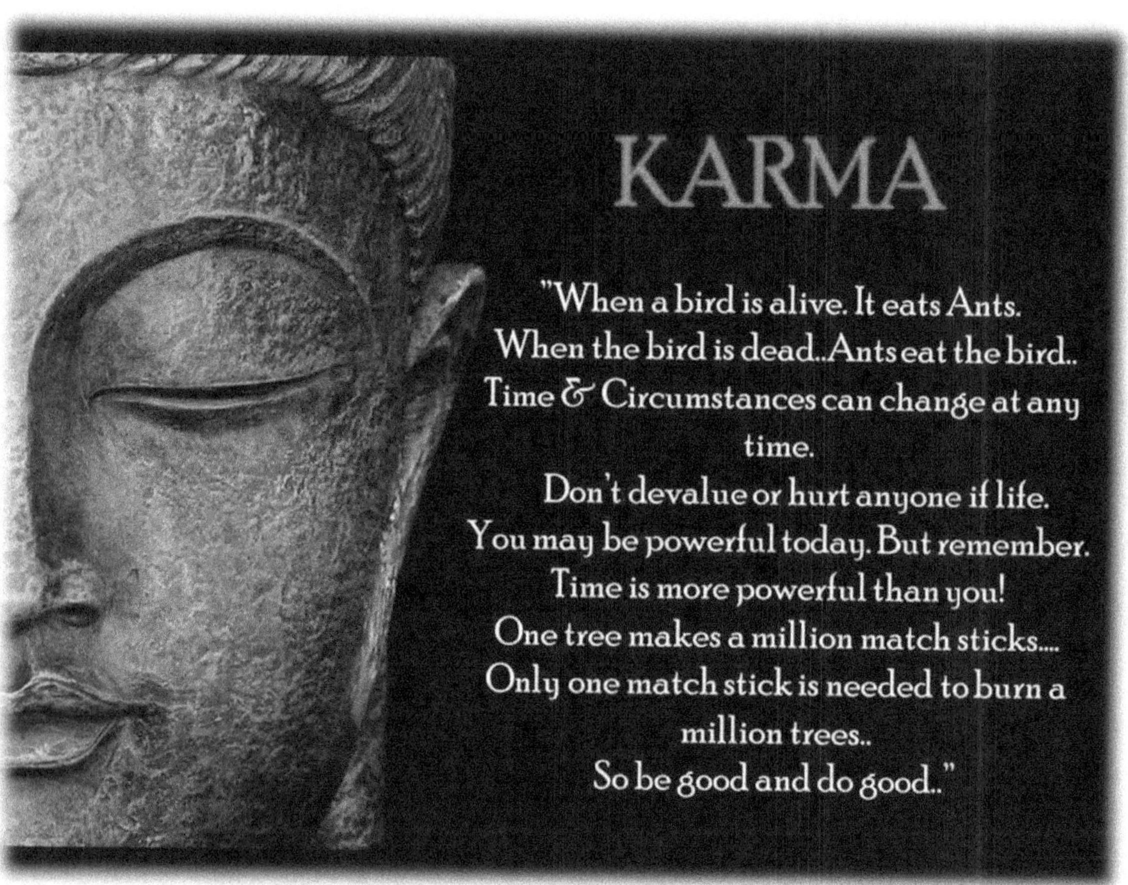

"Shulkin Lied About Purge Authority, White House Protects VA Subversives"

By Benjamin Krause, J.D., March 5, 2018, *DisabledVeterans.org*

In the above article by attorney and investigative reporter Mr. Krause, he wrote that per reports, Shulkin lied about receiving authority from the White House to purge VA employees.

The European travel scandal began to take on, a life of its own. If Shulkin would have immediately apologized and reimbursed the federal taxpayers' their money, the whole story might have blown over within a few days. However, initially, Shulkin was stubborn. He denied wrongdoing. He counter-attacked. He tried to divert attention. It appeared as if his actions <u>after</u> the scandal broke in the news media, are what led to his downfall.

And as if things were not bad enough for Dr. Shulkin, on March 7, 2018, the Office of Inspector General released yet another report to the public that made Secretary Shulkin look yet worse. An official 158-page report outlined extensively and in detail, patient care shortcomings at the VA Medical Center in Washington DC. That VA facility is in the back yard of the Secretary's office. The comprehensive findings of that report are beyond the scope of this book to explain in detail. The bottom line, the problems at the Washington DC VA Medical Center occurred during Shulkin's watch. There is no disputing that. The report added fuel to the fire, well; to fire Shulkin.

"VA Secretary is on Political Life Support after Devastating Inspector General Report Says He Did NOTHING to Fix Danger Hospital in D.C."

By Associated Press and Ariel Zilber for *Dailymail.com*, March 7, 2018

This was a lose-lose situation for the veterans. The longer the scandal went on, the longer the focus remained on the outrage and cover ups, instead of concentrating on the veterans.

Shulkin surged into action moved forward with his strategy to purge the people who reported wrongdoing. To purge the employees who've made him look bad.

"John Ullyot Put on Extended Vacation after Failed Coup of VA Secretary"

By Benjamin Krause, March 9, 2018, *DisabledVeterans.org*

John Ullyot is the Assistant Secretary of Veterans Affairs for Public and Intergovernmental Affairs. Basically, Mr. Ullyot is responsible for managing the news that comes out of the VA. Per the agency's web site, www.va.gov, below is a copy and paste.

"He plays a critical role in guiding VA's public and internal communications strategies and engagements."[2]

Ullyot was making suggestions how to improve the VA and then reportedly was encouraging Shulkin's ouster because he felt the Secretary was not doing the best job possible for the veterans.

Unless Shulkin is put in check by the White House, Mr. Ullyot could be the first salvo of VA employees at the central office in Washington DC to be purged because he did not see eye-to-eye with Shulkin.

John Ullyot

"A War Inside the VA is Paralyzing Trump's Plan to Fix Veterans' Care"

By Lisa Rein, March 9, 2018, *The Washington Post*

The above article by Ms. Rein, does a good job touching on the critical points in a chronological order to describe how we got to this point. The article reports that Shulkin wants to purge at least six members of his senior team.

The Department of Veterans Affairs is the second largest department in the federal government, more than 350,000 employees and the 2019 proposed budget of $200 billion dollars. In Ms. Rein's article is the following copy and paste. *"Things have come to a grinding halt,"* one senior manager said. *"It's killing the agency. Nobody trusts each other."*

The Department of Veterans Affairs has a long history of dysfunction. But it seems as if Shulkin has guided it to an unprecedented degree of chaos.

Are you thinking this is out of control? Well just wait. Then this happened.

"VA Secretary David Shulkin has an <u>Armed</u> <u>Guard</u> Outside His Office to Protect Him from His Own Staff"

By Kimberly Alters, March 9, 2018, *TheWeek.com*

Things had gotten so out of control, that Shulkin was managing the VA from his fortified office/bunker in Washington DC. Multiple news reports stated that Shulkin cancelled meetings with his senior management team because he did not trust them.

<u>Essential Question</u>: How can a leader run an efficient and effective department when he refuses to meet with his senior staff; and doesn't even trust them anyhow?

<u>Fundamental Question</u>: Will the whistleblowers who got purged during the David Shulkin three-year tour of duty, be re-hired?

Lordy, I hope there are tapes - so that there will be accountability.

David finally realizes the game is over

Draining the VA SWAMP

<u>Prediction</u>: David Shulkin will hear the words, you're fired, by the end of March 2018.

<u>Prediction</u>: Even though several names have been floated in the news media about Shulkin's successor, I'm doubtful President Trump will select one of them.

I expect President Trump to nominate someone who he personally knows, respects and has a medical and military background. The President might want someone who knows his way around Washington (but not part of the current VA leadership), to make it easier for that individual to navigate the politics that is unfortunately part of being a successful Secretary of the Department of Veterans Affairs. But someone who is not part of the Establishment, so they will have a better chance of confirmation by the Senate. Confirmation in 2018, an election year, could be a particularly nasty experience. So, someone who is relatively apolitical would be advantageous to get confirmed. Someone like his personal physician would meet those criteria.

Hmmm…

---

[1] https://www.merriam-webster.com/dictionary/karma

[2] https://www.va.gov/opa/bios/bio_ullyot.asp

Editorial Unfiltered

"No need for revenge. Just sit back and wait. Those who hurt you will eventually screw up themselves and if you're lucky, God will let you watch."

Author Unknown

Source: Greg Kearney with permission
Cartoon appeared in the Billings Gazette on February 18, 2018 regarding VA retaliation against dentist Dr. Kelly Hale.

As reported in *Scandals: Unmasking the Underbelly of the VA,* published January 2018, after Kelly Hale, D.D.S. reported substandard care, his dental clinic was abruptly closed. As of the publication date of this book, Dr. Hale continues to be sequestered in solitary confinement for more than 13 continuous months, without assigned duties, but retains his annual VA salary of approximately $200,000 dollars, including full benefits, despite seeing no patients.

During Secretary David Shulkin's 3-year tour of duty with the VA, many whistleblowers were purged, including this author. Whistleblowers think "purge" is just Shulkin's politically correct name for "retaliate". Reminder, after Hitler seized power, the Nazis began purging Germany of Jews.

Whistleblowers have known for a long time the VA, to include Shulkin, were not protecting us. After the European travel scandal was unmasked, Shulkin verbalized his desire to "purge".

<u>Ethical Question</u>: Did prostituting ethics (iCARE values) for self-gratifying rewards take place, which eventually led to purge the messenger mentality?

The following facts were attained from the VA's web site on March 15, 2018.

3,481 VA employees were removed, suspended or demoted from January 20, 2017 through February 14, 2018.[1]

Department of Veterans Affairs
Purge Report

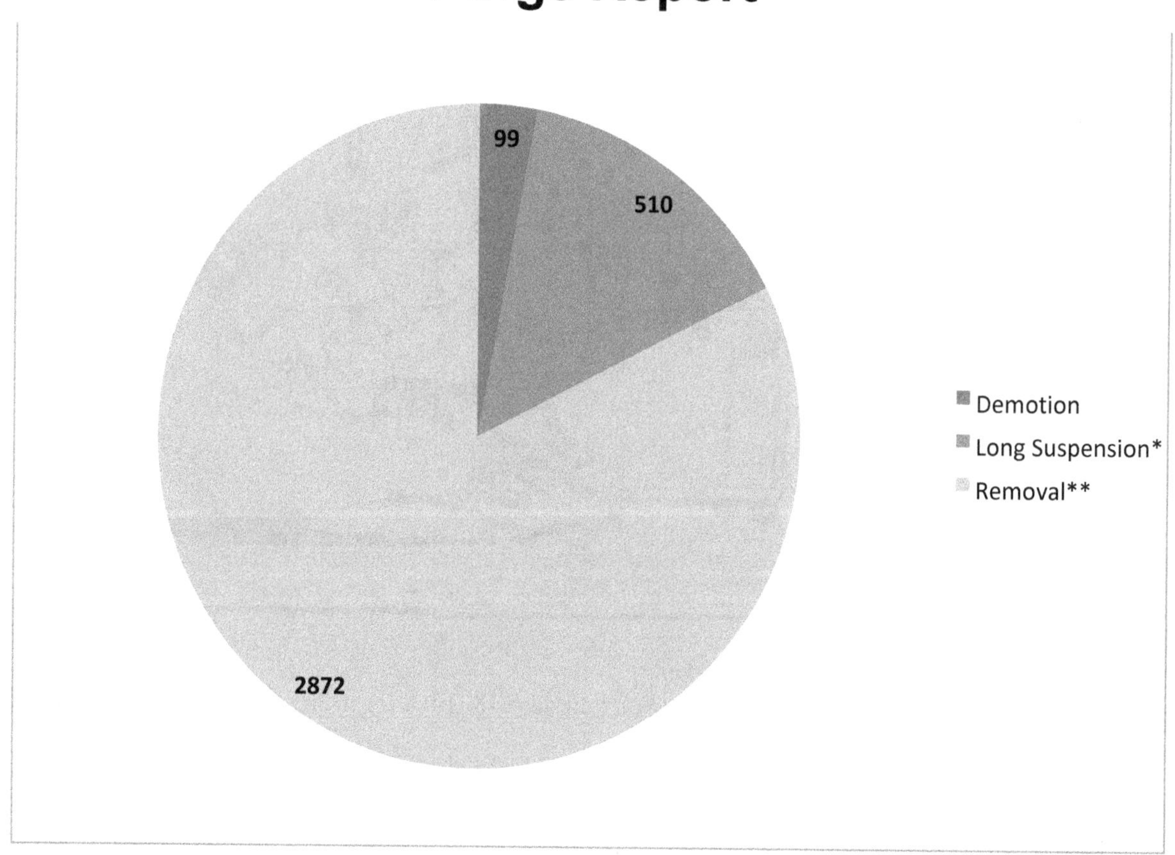

Silencing whistleblowers

Consequently, the habit of purging VA employees pleads attention and corrective action. During David Shulkin's three years in leadership positions with the VA, all whistleblowers who were retaliated against and fired/purged, at a minimum, should have their termination proceedings re-evaluated to determine if discharge was valid!

The content of this book is food for thought. The VA symbolizes a large profligate corporation, with the described European travel to multiple foreign countries on the taxpayers' dime and retaliating against and firing whistleblowers, representative scandals. After reading this book, if you think VA leadership is a son-of-a- , please reflect on the following.

The Bible says in the gospel according to Matthew,[2] regarding passing judgement.

Do not judge, or you too will be judged. For in the same way you judge others, you will be judged, and with the measure you use, it will be measured to you.

Matthew 7:1-2

If you concluded VA leadership did wrong, consider reinforcing your own ethics that you will not do such hateful and vengeful behavior in your life.

----

[1] https://va.gov/accountability/Adverse Actions Report.pdf

[2] Bible: The Gospel according to Matthew, Chapter 7, Verses 1 and 2

Acknowledgements

Thank you to the countless reporters who cover VA stories, some of which I've referenced in this paperback. My book is based on those accounts reported in the news media. Journalists have the unique influence to effect significant positive change on a national level.

Links

Source: Brian Narelle with permission

VA Truth Tellers
https://www.facebook.com/VA.Truth.Tellers

Whistleblowers of America
https://whistleblowersofamerica.org

Stop Military Medical Negligence
http://www.stopmilitarymedicalnegligence.org

Joint Commission
https://www.jointcommission.org/report_a_complaint.aspx

White House
https://www.whitehouse.gov/contact

Office of Accountability and Whistleblower Protection
https://va.gov/accountability

VA Office of Inspector General
https://www.va.gov/oig

United States Office of Special Counsel
https://osc.gov

**United States Department of Labor
Occupational Safety and Health Administration**
https://www.osha.gov/workers/file_complaint.html

United States Drug Enforcement Administration
https://www.dea.gov

Homeland Security and Governmental Affairs Committee
https://www.hsgac.senate.gov

House Committee on Veterans Affairs
https://veterans.house.gov

United States Office of Government Ethics
https://www.oge.gov

United States Department of Justice
https://www.justice.gov

Federal Bureau of Investigations
https://www.fbi.gov

United States Equal Employment Opportunity Commission
https://www.eeoc.gov

Government Accountability Project
https://www.whistleblower.org

Disabled Veterans Organization
http://www.disabledveterans.org

Whistleblower Law Firm
http://khawamlaw.com